No One Is Coming

Mastering the ability to live through dark moments by understanding the finished work of Christ

Dominique McDaniel

No One is Coming
by Dominique McDaniel

www.dominiquemcdaniel.com
info@dominiquemcdaniel.com

Published by
www.anointedfirehouse.com
Cover Design by Oladimeji Alaka
Author photograph by Ethan Lens
www.ethanlens.com

ISBN-13: 978-1-955557-08-5

I have tried to recreate events, locales and conversations from my memories of them. In order to maintain their anonymity in some instances, I have changed the names of individuals and places and I may have changed some identifying characteristics and details such as physical properties, occupations and places of residence.

Dedication

I dedicate this book to my mom.
Her life, her legacy, her smile, her voice, her energy, her encouragement are all memorable. For me, in this time of establishing my own legacy, I have learned to value what you left us even more. I hope this book makes you proud!
Mom, I love you!

Acknowledgments

To my husband: Thank you for being super supportive and always pushing me to be greater.

To my parents: Thank you for always being the most amazing parents. You both have poured great wisdom into me and taught me to build my life on things eternal. I'm so grateful for you both!

To my siblings: Thank you all for challenging me and never letting me be mediocre.

To Apostle Bryan Meadows and Pastor Patrice Meadows: You both have been great friends and awesome Pastors. You have stretched me. I remember when Apostle spoke a word over my life in 2014. That word still resonates with me to this day. He said that God was going to use my mind for more than statistics. You both are loved and appreciated so much!

To My Publisher: Thank you for the amazing work you have done and for helping push this book to the next level.

Table of Contents

Introduction

There is a person seated in a dark room behind a door in a broken place. This person is crying, and this person has a great desire for someone to come and comfort or hear his or her heart. This person is in the fetal position and can barely catch their breath through the tears. Then, there is the realization that NO ONE IS COMING. The emptiness will not be filled, and no one will break down this door. However, there is One who already came and completed this process, someone who saw the end and knew their beginning.

This book will help you to navigate through the obstacles of fear, doubt, pain, transition, and loneliness. These are the emotions that most times keep us from going to the next level. Oftentimes, people are lost in the transitions of life because they are waiting for someone else to come and do the work that has already been completed. If this is you, this book will give you the tools to help you agree with and access the finished work of Christ for your Life. This book will be life-changing; it will move you from that fetal position to your place of authority.

Chapter 1

(The Fetal Position)

Again, there is a person in a dark room seated behind a door; this person is holding his or her legs and have tears running down his or her face. He or she is crying loudly, both internally and externally. This person's soul is screaming, and the individual's face looks like a torrential out-pour of rain. This person knows he or she has work to do and a life to live, but it is almost as if everything has stopped and there is no way out of this issue. This person is in the fetal position and can barely catch his or her breath or see through the tears. A part of this person's soul deeply wishes that someone would come to console him or her, and hear his or her heart regarding what is going on with the individual's life, but again, there is the realization that NO ONE IS COMING. The pain of this truth is almost unbearable.

This person is me; this person is you. This person was all of us at some point in our lives. I remember the night before my mom passed. We got the call that she was in hospice, and she was not doing well. She had already been through a twelve-year battle with cancer; some years had been better than others.

The journey started while I was in my sophomore year at college. At the time, my siblings and I did not quite understand what a cancer diagnosis meant or anything about being terminally ill. There was the diagnosis, a quick procedure, and then she came home and lived. So, we figured everything was okay and there was nothing to be concerned with after this.

Six years later, I moved to Indiana to work after graduate school. That's when my mom received a second diagnosis of breast cancer. This time, she would do a few rounds of chemotherapy, and then return to her normal life. At this point, we still did not have a deep understanding of what she was fighting with, but we eventually lost more people to sickness and have had more hospital visits before we came to understand that cancer is not a joke.

I recall on one of my mom's visits to Indiana, she was taking a shower and we thought that her port (place on the body where the chemotherapy is administered) was bleeding. There was brown liquid all over the bathroom. She made a quick call to the doctor and quickly learned that the liquid was just fluid buildup. This was my first realization that this journey was deeper than a simple fix; that's when I realized that her sickness could do more damage than we'd imagined.

Two years after my mom's visit to Indiana, I received a call that she was in the hospital and the doctors were now saying she had stage four lung cancer. The ER doctor was telling her to go to hospice and just wait to die. I got the call directly from my mother. When she called, I was getting ready to go take a midterm exam for a class; I was in graduate school at the time. The pain from that call left me in the fetal position. That's when the reality of life hit me. I was already down about taking the exam, now I had the added fear of losing my mom. What was a girl to do? I cried and cried, but to no avail because no one came. Eventually, my mom and I got better, but that did not change the fact that No ONE CAME. My mom continued to live, even though the doctors said she should go to hospice. Mom continued for three years beyond what the doctors suggested.

This season of my life continued to be challenging. For the next three years, my mom would go in and out of the hospital. That was until I received that final call that my mom was going to hospice. That night, I remember going into prayer, but also being in that fetal position again. I wrestled with the Holy Spirit for most of the night, and then decided that the time was right to let my mom go.

Here I was again, the person at the start of the chapter in tears, barely able to breathe.

My mom was my best friend and biggest encourager. I was broken, but the Holy Spirit gave me insight and clarity on the situation. I was in the fetal position this time, but I was not alone; there was One who got in the fire with me, and this time was different. After being broken, the Lord blessed me, and when I got up from that place, I immediately felt better. My circumstance did not change; my mom still passed away, but almost immediately, I was able to feel the pressure of the situation lift and the strength of the Lord became my portion. We will discuss this transaction in the chapters to come.

Life can bring us to a fetal position through many different types of situations. There are even examples in the Bible where people were brought to this place of distress and were looking for others to be in this place of pain with them. After time went on in the Old Testament, God stepped into many situations by getting in the fire with them or speaking a word of instruction. In the New Testament, we came to recognize the realization that there was a need for Jesus, the Christ, to go to the cross. Him laying His life down on the cross gave Him victory over every low place in our lives and the lives of others.

Let us look at one of the main examples in the Bible. Elijah, the prophet, had just experienced one of his most powerful moments in dealing with the prophets of Baal. After this, he got word from Jezebel through one of her servants that she was going to kill him. After he heard this, fear folded him up until he found himself in a fetal position ready to die and be done with his purpose. He basically said, "Lord, enough is enough." Life was hitting him hard, even though he was operating from a place of authority. Have you ever felt this on your journey? Maybe you were in a high place utilizing your God-given authority when suddenly, you received word of something horrendous heading your way. Consequently, you lost sight of the high place. I think in these times, we say something like, "This is too much!"

Take a look at the scriptures below:

> *Ahab reported to Jezebel everything that Elijah had done, including the massacre of the prophets. Jezebel immediately sent a messenger to Elijah with her threat: "The gods will get you for this and I'll get even with you! By this time tomorrow you'll be as dead as any one of those prophets."*
>
> *When Elijah saw how things were, he ran for dear life to Beersheba, far in the south of Judah. He left his young servant there and then went on into the desert another day's journey. He came to a lone broom bush and collapsed in its shade, wanting in the worst way to be done with it all—to just die: "Enough of this, God! Take my life—I'm ready to join my ancestors in the grave!" Exhausted, he fell asleep under the lone broom bush (message version).*
>
> *~I Kings 19:1-5*

Elijah was someone who had a relationship with the Lord and was doing the work of the Lord. Somehow, his fears about the message, doubts about himself, and the difficulty of the situation got in the way.

Let us dig into Elijah's story a little more. Elijah was a prophet. A prophet is someone who, simply put, shares the heart and mind of God to uplift God's people. He spent most of his time living in a desert place; that was until God called him to Israel. He was sourcing from a river in the desert, but that river eventually dried up. The Lord told him to go visit the home of a widow, promising that she would give him food.

Elijah was then told to confront the king at the time, which was Ahab. Many of us know the story of Ahab and his wife, Jezebel. She is infamous for being controlling, manipulative and just crazy. People often reference someone who has these types of characteristics as a Jezebel. So, Elijah went to let Ahab know that he was the cause of Israel's issues because of his connection to Baal. Elijah challenged the prophets of Baal to call on their god to see if their god could do what they'd ask of him. Here is the passage of scriptures below:

> *Then said Elijah unto the people, I, even I only, remain a prophet of the Lord; but Baal's prophets are four hundred and fifty men. Let them therefore give us two bullocks; and let them choose one bullock for themselves, and cut it in pieces, and lay it on wood, and put no fire under: and I will dress the other bullock, and lay it on wood, and put no fire under: And call ye on the name of your gods, and I will call on the name of the Lord: and the God that answered by fire, let him be God. And all the people answered and said, It is well spoken. And Elijah said unto the prophets of Baal, Choose you one bullock for yourselves, and dress it first; for ye are many; and call on the name of your gods, but put no fire under. And they took the bullock which was given them, and they dressed it, and called on the name of Baal from morning even until*

> *noon, saying, O Baal, hear us. But there was no voice, nor any that answered. And they leaped upon the altar which was made. And it came to pass at noon, that Elijah mocked them, and said, Cry aloud: for he is a god; either he is talking, or he is pursuing, or he is in a journey, or peradventure he sleepeth, and must be awaked.*
>
> *~I Kings 18:22-27*

Elijah then has this powerful moment where he was able to demonstrate to the four hundred and fifty prophets of Baal who the real God is. He is the God who can and would answer by fire. After this victory, he received the news that Jezebel was planning to have him killed. Elijah then found himself in a fearful place, wanting his life to end after hearing this message. This is where we find Elijah in the fetal position. He'd allowed his fears, doubts, and worries to get the best of him. He found himself in the place of the person I mentioned at the start of this chapter. This is where most of us end up while pursuing purpose. In the low places, we have experienced great deals of pain and trauma; this is the time and the place when we find ourselves longing for someone to come and rescue us. However, no one shows up, and in Elijah's case, he was fed and told to get back to work.

Most of us know the fetal position as it relates to babies. While babies are in the womb, the safest position for them is the fetal position. The fetal position is when babies make a C-shape, with a curved spine, head down, while their arms and legs are pulled close to their bodies, touching their torsos. Adults, make a similar shape when they get into the fetal position, but typically, this is due to stress or trauma. Normally, adults may get in this position to protect their brains or organs from injuries. This especially occurs when the brain is no longer able to cope with the environment and has basically had enough.

There was an article in Psychology Today that mentioned five ways that body language can signal trouble. This article listed number three as the fetal position. Basically, when hearing news or an event overwhelms an adult, it can cause them to drop into the fetal position. Also, people who deal with anxiety or panic issues will often find themselves in the fetal position.

While we may see the fetal position as a place of pain and a way to deal with stress and trauma, we also know that anything the Lord breaks, He also has a plan to bless. We see this in Luke 9:16 when He broke the bread before blessing it. Again, the principle established is—anything God breaks, He blesses.

You may be in a season where you feel the weight of your environment, and this has caused you to constantly put yourself in the fetal position. Please understand that you can get into the fetal position both physically and mentally; this happens when you feel the need to protect what is important to you: your heart. Though it may feel like a difficult season, the fetal position is actually the position you have to be in when you are being prepared to be birthed. The broken place is the best place for you to birth everything that God intended for you to birth.

The fetal position is the best position for the fetus because, when the baby's due date arrives, this is the best position for the baby to be birthed. This position helps to lower the risk of complications during the birthing process. During the birthing process, many things will come to distract and pull you away from producing the promises of God in your life. The Lord says today that the low place will keep you out of the enemy's reach. Yes! This season may have caused us to feel stressed, and we may feel tired, but the Holy Spirit sees us and knows our futures. There is a way of escape, and God has pre-planned the route.

So, stay tuned as we go deeper into the understanding of how the finished work of Christ will bring us out of our low places into our heavenly places.

Just speak this to yourself… I am not looking for an earthly savior because my Father in Heaven has already saved me!

> *Humble yourselves in the sight of the Lord, and he shall lift you up.*
>
> *~James 4:10*

Chapter 2

(No One is Coming)

The idea that no one is coming can sound a bit harsh. So, I wanted to take the time to explain exactly what this concept means. Oftentimes, we find ourselves looking for a savior—not Jesus, the Savior, but one who's here with us now. A savior is someone who brings you out of danger or destruction. We are oftentimes looking for someone to pay our bills, help us to lose weight, assist us in writing our books, or get rid of debt for us. Also, we want someone to deal with the pain and the challenging moments for us.

So, let's go back to the picture of the person in the fetal position. Within this individual, there is an internal desire for a savior. I use the word savior because many times, we are looking for a spouse, friend, parent, brother, or sister to come and bear the weight of our situations for us. Some of us are looking for a black Jesus, a white Jesus, or even a baby Jesus to come back and save us again. If someone could just get in the ring with us and take the hits, we would be alright.

When I say that no one is coming, I'm not saying that you will be alone on your journey. I am not throwing away the fact that we need people in our lives. Having great people in our circles is very important in life. I am speaking to the hard places that most people cannot go with us. To the challenging situations that those around us do not understand or only understand to a certain extent. I am speaking to the wife that may feel alone in a matter. I am speaking to the educated person who is the first in his or her family to take the step towards a brighter future, and no one understands the difficulty of the journey. All they can do is praise you for where you are headed. I am speaking to the grieving person who feels like no one can truly understand the pain of whatever it is that's grieving you. I am speaking to the entrepreneur, the one who decided to leave his or her day job and put everything on the line. I am speaking to the one who is caring for a sick loved one to the best of his or her ability. There are many of us facing so many challenging situations. Hear me, there is hope because the One we are looking for already came for us.

Now, let us look at a woman I'll call Lisa. Her life seems to be well put together. She has a nice car, house, and a great job, but her desire is to be a wife and a mother. She has many great qualities that would make her the most amazing wife, but the right man has not come. So, Lisa feels alone; she is hurting because she is not able to accomplish the one thing she desires so deeply. Lisa lights up the life of so many others; she is patient, giving and kind. You can find her on the weekends serving others and you can find her at church on Sundays. There is never a moment where Lisa is not living out her God-given purpose.

Life begins to challenge Lisa in her health. That's when the thoughts begin about her not being married and not having the children she's always desired. The fears of this never happening for her, the doubts about her even being good enough, the pain of not having the person she's always pictured herself with are all too much. These thoughts begin to take over Lisa's mind, and she becomes broken thinking about the fact that what she desires most has not happened yet.

Lisa finds herself ready to give up on everything; she has had enough with life. Everyone sees Lisa as this amazing person, but Lisa does not see herself through that lens. She sees herself through the lens of self-pity. Lisa has great friends, but all they do is remind her of the bank account she has and how they would trade places with her any day of the week. The reminder here is that no one is coming, but then again, someone has already came. That is the person of Jesus, the Christ. He came not to condemn the world, but so that we might be saved. There is so much more to explain here, but we will get there in later chapters. However, there is one example in the Bible worth mentioning.

Do you know the story of Esther? Esther was a Jewish woman. She was married to a Persian king. One day, Esther found herself in the palace, crowned as the queen of Persia. Everything was great until she heard from her cousin, Mordecai, that there had been a decree put out to have the Jews killed. She heard the news and was immediately grieved. This is where we find Esther in the fetal position, ready to give up on everything. She was extremely saddened by this decree; she felt as if she didn't have anyone to talk to or anyone to rely on to get her people out of this situation.

Esther was in a low place. Can you imagine knowing that the deliverance of a generation is on you? I know we declare stuff like this all the time, but do we see the deliverance of our people happening through us in our decisions and in our obedience? I think that we never really look at our obedience in that way. We just make decisions or choose not to obey completely and deal with the consequences. Could you imagine if Esther had decided to just live her life as queen and had not decided to intercede on behalf of God's people? What if Esther stayed in the fetal position and rotted away “waiting on the Lord” or some “savior”? The reason for the quotes is to emphasize the fact that we oftentimes hide behind the concept of waiting on the Lord or praying about a matter. We drag our feet and delay the deliverance of nations and generations because we choose not to be who we were called to be, and we choose to stay in the fetal place.

Here is another one. What if Esther had not responded to Mordecai's plea? Some of us would have reacted in shock to the report or just became emotional, making matters even worse. We would not have spent any time in prayer regarding the matter. Oftentimes, we just talk about how we feel while in the fetal place. It is there that we change our decrees, and we just go with our emotions, basically allowing our emotions to dictate the outcome of the matter. Please remember that Christ, our Savior, has already reported the outcome of every situation regardless of what it looks like. We still have the VICTORY! Because the blood of Jesus still and always will work. Esther had this realization before Christ came into the Earth.

The interesting thing about the book of Esther is that this book of the Bible does not even mention God. So, my girl, Esther, already knew and understood this concept very well. She understood that NO ONE IS COMING, so let's get up from here and be who God called us to be. Let us look at the verses below:

> *When Mordecai perceived all that was done, Mordecai rent his clothes, and put on sackcloth with ashes, and went out into the midst of the city, and cried with a loud and a bitter cry. And came even before the king's gate: for none might enter into the king's gate clothed with sackcloth. And in every province, whithersoever the king's commandment and his decree came, there was great*

mourning among the Jews, and fasting, and weeping, and wailing; and many lay in sackcloth and ashes. So Esther's maids and her chamberlains came and told it her. Then was the queen exceedingly grieved; and she sent raiment to clothe Mordecai, and to take away his sackcloth from him: but he received it not.

~Esther 4:1-4

Esther found herself distraught and broken. She is the person at the start of the book. In the room, no one could hear her cry, but she was crying out loudly. She is we, and we are her. The same system that she was married to was working to kill off her people. Esther decided that enough is enough; she was ready to escape this life or, even worse, turn her back on her people. Her cousin challenged her thoughts. He pretty much said to her, “Listen, I hope you don't think that being in the palace is going to save you. You are still a Jew, and you will not get overlooked.”

Here is why we like Queen Esther. She quickly realized that she had the power within her, plus she realized that NO ONE WAS COMING. She got up from the fetal place and pretty much said, "Look, there is power within me, but I am also going to need supernatural power to go before this king and turn this situation around." Look at the passage below for yourself:

> *Then Mordecai commanded to answer Esther, Think not with thyself that thou shalt escape in the king's house, more than all the Jews. For if thou altogether holdest thy peace at this time, then shall there enlargement and deliverance arise to the Jews from another place; but thou and thy father's house shall be destroyed: and who knoweth whether thou art come to the kingdom for such a time as this? Then Esther bade them return Mordecai this answer, Go, gather together all the Jews that are present in Shushan, and fast ye for me, and neither eat nor drink three days, night or day: I also and my maidens will fast*

likewise; and so will I go in unto the king, which is not according to the law: and if I perish, I perish.

~Esther 4:13-16

Esther is such an amazing example of how life can be challenging but great at the same time. How we can be living our best lives while facing problems that force us to our knees. However, there are ways to face the difficulties of life. All the fears, doubts, worries, grief, and transitions cannot be avoided in life. The beauty of life is that there is One who can go through these situations with us; He has already gone through them for us. Personally, I feel this book of the Bible is incredibly encouraging because God was never mentioned. So, even though we may go through seasons where it feels as if God is not present, He is not hearing us or He is not seeing us, the Lord is always with us and has gone before us.

The queen had to be confident in the very work that the Lord had begun in her and trust that He would be with her to see that work through, even though a part of her journey was facing a pagan king and turning over a decree the king made. What Esther was destined to do could have gotten her killed or had her in prison for years. The very decision to get up from the fetal place and to speak out was the thing that enabled a generation to live. Wow, at this point, have you asked yourself what you have been delaying doing or what decisions you have been putting off that have been holding up the freedom of God's people? As I write these words, I am almost convicted, but I feel this is the perfect time for me to release this book. I may have delayed a bit, but I'm thankful that God did not deny me.

Many of us are looking for miracles, signs, and wonders for us to make the decisions we need to make. And not just any miracle, we are basically looking for Jesus Himself to bring us to the water so we can take a sip (as the older folks would say). We totally miss the millions of miracles that are happening daily, like the fact that we are alive and have some functionality in our bodies. In other words, the time is perfect to say YES, LORD. In the Bible, people have been in situations like the one Esther found herself in, but unlike Esther, they had a sign or at least a mention of God, but Esther had no confirmation. She just had a set of instructions and her commitment to her people. She just had faith to know that God was with her. Many of us are waiting on God to decide for us, when God is waiting on us. Once we make the decision, the Lord will reveal Himself all the more.

The Lord is saying there is nothing wrong with feeling like you are in a low place. Matter of fact, He has called many of us to low places to deal with character issues, such as the children of Israel. The Lord led them to bitter water after they spent three days without water. How crazy does that sound?! The children of Israel were traveling in a desert without water, and the Lord led them to water that was bitter! We do not like to see the Lord this way; we want to see our challenging situations as something the enemy put on our paths. This oftentimes gives the enemy too much power. We can look at the passage of scripture below to see what happened to the children of Israel:

> *So Moses brought Israel from the Red sea, and they went out into the wilderness of Shur; and they went three days in the wilderness, and found no water. And when they came to Marah, they could not drink of the waters of Marah, for they were bitter: therefore the name of it was called Marah.*
> *And the people murmured against Moses, saying, What shall we drink?*
> *And he cried unto the Lord; and the Lord shewed him a tree, which when he had cast into the waters, the waters were made sweet: there he made for them a statute and an ordinance, and there he proved them, And said, If thou wilt diligently hearken to the voice of the Lord thy God, and wilt do that which is right in his sight, and wilt give ear to his commandments, and keep all his*

statutes, I will put none of these diseases upon thee, which I have brought upon the Egyptians: for I am the Lord that healeth thee. And they came to Elim, where were twelve wells of water, and threescore and ten palm trees: and they encamped there by the waters.

~Exodus 15:22-27

So, the children of Israel reacted to the fact that they were at a bitter pool by complaining. This is another issue that many of us have; we complain, rather than have faith and hold onto our decrees in the face of adversity. The children of Israel cried, "What are we going to drink now?! He has taken us out of Egypt, and now we don't have any water! We should have stayed where we were at!" I can almost hear them now, saying things like, "All this walking is too much! Moses up here parting red seas but does not have any clean water for us!" Do you see how a normal conversation can quickly move contrary to your faith and your position in God? The children of

Israel were allowing their fears, doubts, worries, transitions, and pains to get the best of them. A simple, "God, I thank You," could have been enough. Matter of fact, let us take a moment right now just to thank God.

The children of Israel were led to bitter waters where Moses began to pray and cry out to the Lord. Moses was given instructions on how to perform a miracle and turn the waters from bitter into sweet tasting water. At this bitter place, God made a covenant with the children of Israel, saying that if they would obey Him, listen and keep His commandments, they would never see the Egyptians, sickness or disease. Did you hear that? If they obeyed God, there would never be a moment where they would find themselves in the fetal position because they would remain in the presence of God.

The important thing to understand is that God sometimes takes us to low places to bring us to higher places in Him. The right amount of pressure will bring out the character issues that lie deep within us. Those issues may be keeping us from our seated places with the Lord. So, he brings us low so that we can go higher. Better said, He brings us low so that we can get in right-standing or right covenant with Him.

Let's revisit Queen Esther's story. There she was in a palace married to a Persian king. This is a position she should have never been able to get to in life. She was positioned for purpose, and she did not even know this. The fetal position for Esther was a setup for her to be able to birth the deliverance of her people. The low place gave her insight and helped her to see her potential. It was in that low place that she found the strategy she needed to get the king to overturn the judgment he'd made against her people.

She did not wait for a "savior" or spend years saying, "I am praying for the Jews." Esther rose to the occasion, allowing clear decision-making and obedience to direct her path. The queen let the fetal place become her birthing place. This is where she found strength in the face of adversity. She quickly realized that no one was coming because she was the one born for the moment she'd found herself in. The pain and the fear set the stage for the awakening of her own power. She came to understand that she was stronger than she'd thought. Let's take a look at the victory that was achieved through Esther's story:

> *On that day did the king Ahasuerus give the house of Haman the Jews' enemy unto Esther the queen. And Mordecai came before the king; for Esther had told what he was unto her. And the king took off his ring, which he had taken from Haman, and gave it unto Mordecai. And Esther set Mordecai over the house of Haman. And Esther spake yet again before the king, and fell down at his feet, and besought him with tears to put away the mischief of Haman the Agagite, and his device that he had devised against the Jews. Then the king held out the golden sceptre toward Esther. So Esther arose, and stood*

before the king, And said, If it please the king, and if I have favour in his sight, and the thing seem right before the king, and I be pleasing in his eyes, let it be written to reverse the letters devised by Haman the son of Hammedatha the Agagite, which he wrote to destroy the Jews which are in all the king's provinces: For how can I endure to see the evil that shall come unto my people? Or how can I endure to see the destruction of my kindred? Then the king Ahasuerus said unto Esther the queen and to Mordecai the Jew, Behold, I have given Esther the house of Haman, and him they have hanged upon the gallows, because he laid his hand upon the Jews. Write ye also for the Jews, as it liketh you, in the king's name, and seal it with the king's ring: for the writing, which is written in the king's name, and sealed with the king's ring, may no man reverse. Then were the king's scribes called at that time in the third month, that is, the month Sivan, on the three and twentieth day thereof; and it was written according to all that Mordecai commanded unto the Jews, and to the lieutenants, and the deputies and rulers of the provinces which are from India unto Ethiopia, an hundred twenty and seven provinces, unto every province according to the writing thereof, and unto every people after their language, and to the Jews according to their writing, and according to their language. And he wrote in the king Ahasuerus' name, and sealed it with the king's ring, and sent letters by posts on horseback, and riders on mules, camels, and young dromedaries: Wherein the king granted the Jews which were in every city to gather themselves together, and to stand for their life, to destroy, to slay and to cause to perish, all the power of the people and province that would assault them, both little ones and women, and to take the spoil of them for a prey,

Upon one day in all the provinces of king Ahasuerus, namely, upon the thirteenth day of the twelfth month, which is the month Adar.

~Esther 8:1-12

Have you ever felt like Esther? Have you ever had a moment or a season where you were grieved, hurt, or saddened by something that was going on or a message you'd received? Or you may be in that place currently. Have you ever felt like the children of Israel, where you'd gone without something for so long and you just knew the Lord was leading you to a crystal clear well with everything you needed, only to discover that the place He'd led you to seemed to be more challenging than the place you'd left? I just want to encourage and remind you that trouble will not last always and that there is great beauty coming out of this situation. The covenant that we are in with the Lord is more than we could have ever imagined.

Make this confession: I am grateful to be led by You, God, and wherever You lead me, I will follow.

> *In everything give thanks: for this is the will of God in Christ Jesus concerning you.*
>
> *~I Thessalonians 5:18*

Prayer

God, we thank You that we are alive. We thank You that we are breathing and that we are in our right minds. God, we thank You for strength and strategy!

Chapter 3

(The Fears)

Becoming pregnant for the first time is such a joy. If there are no complications, this experience can be one of the most meaningful times of your life. You are making a human; someone is going to exist on the Earth that you have played a role in bringing here. I remember dreaming of the day we would find out the gender of our child. I was so excited to be able to know a little about the person who was going to exist in the Earth because of us. I thought about how we would celebrate while receiving the news and how we'd celebrate afterwards. The room would light up the moment we discovered our child's gender, and someone would have a microphone to announce the news to our loved ones. Next, there would be dancing and screaming, and after that, we would go out for the most amazing dinner and just dream about the baby to come.

Instead, the woman performing the ultrasound made us wait anxiously for about an hour while she went through every detail of our baby's organs. We were ready to fall asleep as she pointed out a bunch of organs that we could not identify through the screen. She then said in the most monotone and dry voice, "You are having a boy." I was extremely sad after she left the room because I felt like she'd ruined our moment. I'm not sure what had potentially ruined her day, but this was nothing like what I'd expected to happen in one of the most notable moments of our lives. After she left the room, I shed a few tears because I felt she'd missed the mark, but I had no idea of what was to come for the rest of the day.

So, we left the appointment happy but equally disappointed, and trying to figure out what was next. We also wondered how we were going to share the news with our folks, and what we were going to eat. (Note: We decide on tacos at one of our favorite places.) We brought ourselves back together and decided who we would tell first. We began making the calls. We called our dads first, and after that, my husband called his mother. That's when grief hit me like a ton of bricks. I had never cried that much since my mom passed, but right there in the middle of that restaurant, those welled-up tears began to flow. I could not stop to explain the reasoning for the tears; all I could do was feel the intensity of the pain I was in. I could never call my mom and tell her what gender the baby was or even that we were having a baby. She would never meet him in person; we would never get to experience generational photos or videos. My mind began to flood with thoughts of all the moments my mom would miss because she was no longer with us.

There, we were on one of the greatest days of our lives about halfway through the pregnancy, now knowing a baby boy was joining our family, but all I could feel was the pain of grief in every part of my body. I could hear the conversations my mom and I used to have about how she would come spend six months of every year with us whenever I had a baby, especially the first few months after delivery. She told me that she would do the cleaning and the cooking (healthy cooking that is), and all we had to do was take care of the baby. She would talk about her being at the hospital with a million outfits, even though the baby would not need any of them. My mom was very determined to outdo her mom when she had me. I could also laugh amid crying because I could also hear her jokes about how our baby would come out and be a nerd; she joked that he would have glasses that were banded around his head. Also, she would say that we were going to name our first child DarDom, a combination of our first names. Mom was quite the comedian.

On this day, I once again felt like the person in chapter one, however, this felt different. There was an actual hole in my life, and there was no one around who could fill that space. While there are many people who have supported me through my mom's transition, most people who are grieving or have grieved the loss of a parent know that you may move forward, but you never want to move on. I may connect with women that have motherly like abilities, but I would never use them to replace my mother.

There I was in the dark room again in the fetal position, crying and screaming, but this time, the biggest voice or emotion I felt was fear. Fear gripped me; that is, fear of the future, fear of life without my mother, fear of failure, fear of rejection, and fear of death. Each of these fears communicated with me by sharing visual images of the challenges that were ahead of me, because of the pain that was behind me. I pictured myself rocking my baby while he was crying, and no one would be there to support me or walk me through what to do next.

This all started with a pure emotion of grief; this is a moment that we are allowed to live in for a space of time. Fear brought a few friends with it: anxiety and rejection. After this, a slippery slope began to form that would prove to be difficult to recover from. This is the downward spiral of grief. The more images that form in our minds of the difficulties ahead, the further we slide down the mountain until we are in the valley of despair, hopeless and holding our knees against our chest.

In this space of uncertainty, many invisible enemies will try to speak to us to exacerbate our situations. This is what makes the low place complicated. An event happens and causes us to be in the pit, and then fear, pain, doubt, loneliness, and other enemies come to add to the misery of the matter. For example, if someone had a miscarriage, the thoughts would come about that person not being able to get pregnant again or not being able to carry full-term. What if you were broken and could never be fixed to the standard you think you need to be? These thoughts are rooted in fear. Fear comes in many ways, sizes, shapes, and forms.

What is fear? Fear, by definition, is an emotion that is driven by a perceived threat. This can cause a psychological change, which can ultimately become a behavioral change. Fear is oftentimes activated by an image or an imagination of potential physical or psychological danger, both present or futuristic. The existence of fear causes an emotional and/or biochemical response in our bodies. A biochemical response can be having the sweats, an increased heart rate or an increase in our adrenaline levels. Emotional responses can be similar to biochemical responses, however, our emotions can be driven by positive or negative fear experiences. Some people may experience fear because they are thrill-seekers, while others may be in a more negative situation. In addition to these responses, there are several symptoms caused by fear, which can include: chest pain, chills, nausea, and shortness of breath. Lastly, fear can be caused by our imaginations of future events, imagined events, the unknown, real environmental dangers, or certain objects or situations.

In a more practical way, we can identify fear by evaluating ourselves. If we ask ourselves introspective questions, it would be easier for us to identify our fears. We should ask ourselves questions like:

- What are we thinking about?
- What are our primary beliefs?
- What is the source of those beliefs?

For example, when you get a call late at night from a family member, what is your first thought and why do you have that idea? Do you immediately think someone is in danger? Do you go down a trail of thoughts, thinking of all the evil things that could have happened? The source of this type of thinking is fear.

Now, unchecked fear can become anxiety. The distinction between fear and anxiety is this: fear is the initial idea, but what we do with the thought can become anxiety. If we wallow in the initial thought and allow further subsequent thoughts on the topic, that becomes anxiety. For example, if we have our initial thought that someone is in danger because we received a call late at night, we could take two paths from there. We could speak against that thought and interrupt it with a scripture. The other path is, we could start to think about the different dangers that have occurred or could potentially occur, and we can come up with a whole imagined event in our heads.

To consider the proverbial "train of thought," consider this scenario: Barry gets a call at one in the morning from one of his children. He immediately thinks that his child has been hurt. The next thought he has is that she has been kidnapped and taken hostage, and the person on the other end of the line is calling for ransom. Barry starts to experience cold chills and he begins to sweat profusely. He has not even heard from his child yet, but he has a whole event playing over and over in his head.

Our minds know how to play tricks on us and lead us down some slippery slopes. The key piece is that our minds belong to us. This gives us the responsibility of managing our minds. Philippians 2:5 says, "Let this mind be in you, which was also in Christ Jesus." This verse gives us a great piece of instruction if we focus on the word "let." Let, in this verse, is telling us that there is a decision to be made on our parts; we must allow the mind of Christ to be in us. There is a need for us to come into agreement with the type of mindset that Christ has for us to overcome this slippery slope our minds may try to take us on.

Jesus' mind possesses so many excellent characteristics, one of which is faith. Faith is a key tool to combat fear. Faith, by definition, is complete trust in someone or something. Our complete trust in God drives out fear as we fill our minds with the Word of the Lord. Many people in the Bible had a struggle with fear versus faith. One person I immediately think about is Moses.

This passage of scripture shares with us about Moses' conversation with God where he put his fears over his faith:

And Moses answered and said, But, behold, they will not believe me, nor hearken unto my voice: for they will say, The Lord hath not appeared unto thee.

And the Lord said unto him, What is that in thine hand? And he said, A rod.

And he said, Cast it on the ground. And he cast it on the ground, and it became a serpent; and Moses fled from before it.

And the Lord said unto Moses, Put forth thine hand, and take it by the tail. And he put forth his hand, and caught it, and it became a rod in his hand: That they may believe that the Lord God of their fathers, the God of Abraham, the God of Isaac, and the God of Jacob, hath appeared unto thee. And the Lord said furthermore unto him, Put now thine hand into thy bosom. And he put his hand into his bosom: and when he took it out, behold, his hand was leprous as snow. And he said, Put thine hand into thy bosom again. And he put his hand into his bosom again; and plucked it out of his bosom, and, behold, it was turned again as his other flesh. And it shall come to pass, if they will not believe thee, neither hearken to the voice of the first sign, that they will believe the voice of the latter sign. And it shall come to pass, if they will not believe also these two signs, neither hearken unto thy voice, that thou shalt take of the water of the river and pour it upon the dry land: and the water which thou takest out of the river shall become blood upon the dry land. And Moses said unto the Lord, O my Lord, I am not eloquent, neither heretofore, nor since thou hast spoken unto thy servant: but I am slow of speech, and of a slow tongue. And the Lord said unto him, Who hath made man's mouth? or who maketh the dumb, or deaf, or the seeing, or the blind? have not I the Lord? Now therefore go, and I will be with thy mouth, and teach thee what thou shalt say. And he said, O my Lord, send, I pray thee, by the hand of him whom thou wilt send. And the anger of the Lord was kindled against Moses, and he said, Is not Aaron the

Levite thy brother? I know that he can speak well. And also, behold, he cometh forth to meet thee: and when he seeth thee, he will be glad in his heart. And thou shalt speak unto him, and put words in his mouth: and I will be with thy mouth, and with his mouth, and will teach you what ye shall do. And he shall be thy spokesman unto the people: and he shall be, even he shall be to thee instead of a mouth, and thou shalt be to him instead of God. And thou shalt take this rod in thine hand, wherewith thou shalt do signs.

~Exodus 4:1-17

How many of us have felt like Moses? God was trying to give us instructions, but we responded with our fears. Moses had five main fears that came to mind while having a conversation with God. He thought he was not good enough, could not speak, did not have all the answers, people would not believe him, and he did not feel qualified. This has been me in times' past. God has given me clear instructions regarding some of the situations I've found myself in, and instead of me trusting Him, I let one of fear's representatives show up in me. I then began to give God a list of why He should not be choosing me.

Moses thought he had the situation figured out by letting God know that his fears outweighed his assignment. He figured God would let him off the hook. God said no, I will give you someone to speak for you, but you will still have to take responsibility and complete the assignment. In this case, the Lord sent someone to help Moses speak, that was his older brother, Aaron. However, while Moses was able to lean on his brother to talk to the people, this did not take away from Moses having to face his fears and still be who God called him to be. Regardless of how he felt, Moses still had to perform the miracles, lead the people out of Egypt, and be the mediator between God and His people.

The thought that someone else was coming to deal with the issue probably crossed his mind many times, but there was something that rose up in Moses when he saw the Hebrew getting hit by an Egyptian. Moses realized early that he was not an Egyptian, even though he did not know his complete story. So, he killed the Egyptian that was hitting the Hebrew. The next day, he broke up a disagreement between two Hebrews, and one said, "Are you going to kill me like you did the Egyptian?" After this, Moses was afraid; he realized that the news had likely reached Pharaoh. Moses ran to Midian and sat down by a well. Check out the passage of scriptures below:

> *And it came to pass in those days, when Moses was grown, that he went out unto his brethren, and looked on their burdens: and he spied an Egyptian smiting an Hebrew, one of his brethren. And he looked this way and that way, and when he saw that there was no man, he slew the Egyptian, and hid him in the sand. And when he went out the second day, behold, two men of the Hebrews strove together: and he said to*

him that did the wrong, Wherefore smitest thou thy fellow? And he said, Who made thee a prince and a judge over us? intendest thou to kill me, as thou killedst the Egyptian? And Moses feared, and said, Surely this thing is known. Now when Pharaoh heard this thing, he sought to slay Moses. But Moses fled from the face of Pharaoh and dwelt in the land of Midian: and he sat down by a well.

~Exodus 2:11-15

This fact is important to point out in many biblical characters, so that we will realize how we are connected to them. What do you think Moses was doing at the well in Midian? You got the idea! He was in the fetal position, looking for a savior, allowing his fears to speak to him loudly. Can you imagine Moses lying by the side of the well, holding his knees to his chest, not knowing what was next, but knowing that one of the most powerful people in the world at the time was looking to kill him?

Take a deeper look at the childhood of Moses to understand more about his story. This passage of scripture explains Moses' upbringing and how that set him up to be the leader of the children of Israel:

> *And there went a man of the house of Levi, and took to wife a daughter of Levi. And the woman conceived, and bare a son: and when she saw him that he was a goodly child, she hid him three months. And when she could not longer hide him, she took for him an ark of bulrushes, and daubed it with slime and with pitch, and put the child therein; and she laid it in the flags by the river's brink. And his sister stood afar off, to wit what would be done to him. And the daughter of Pharaoh came down to wash herself at the river; and her maidens walked along by the river's side; and when she saw the ark among the flags, she sent her maid to fetch it. And when she had opened it, she saw the child: and, behold, the babe wept. And she had compassion on him, and*

said, This is one of the Hebrews' children. Then said his sister to Pharaoh's daughter, Shall I go and call to thee a nurse of the Hebrew women, that she may nurse the child for thee? And Pharaoh's daughter said to her, Go. And the maid went and called the child's mother. And Pharaoh's daughter said unto her, Take this child away, and nurse it for me, and I will give thee thy wages. And the woman took the child, and nursed it. And the child grew, and she brought him unto Pharaoh's daughter, and he became her son. And she called his name Moses: and she said, Because I drew him out of the water.

~Exodus 2:1-10

Moses was born in adversity but born for an important time. For the first three months of his life, his mother had to hide him. After hiding him, his mom was forced to put him in a basket in the river to protect him. This is because Pharaoh had given instructions to kill every male baby birthed by the Hebrews. The strategy his mom came up with was to put him in a basket and allow him to float down the river. Moses' sister, Miriam, followed him as he floated in the river. She did this so that she could inform his mother about where he ended up. Somehow, Moses ended up at Pharoah's house; this was the very person who had given the Egyptians instructions to kill him. Pharoah's daughter was captivated by Moses and took him in as her child. Miriam then went to get her mom so that she could nurse the baby for Pharaoh's daughter; this is how he became her son.

Moses ended up growing up in Pharaoh's house, so he learned all the systems, structures, and strategies of the Egyptians. Eventually, Moses realized that he was not an Egyptian; he was a Hebrew. At some point, Moses took the time to visit the Hebrew people. That's when he learned how the Hebrews were being treated. That's when he found himself in a low place, prompting him to kill an Egyptian after seeing the pressure the slave had been put under by the system.

Can you connect with the story of Moses? Can you imagine being born in a time where everything in the world is trying to kill you? Your parents did the best they could with raising you, but there is still a deep feeling of rejection and abandonment. Your mom and/or your dad were trying to protect you in the time you grew up in, but their decisions somehow ended up affecting you negatively. Maybe, you were not raised by your biological parents, but the system that was intended to harm you ended up raising you.

Some of us have deep-rooted trauma that has caused us to build up certain walls because of our fears and apprehensions. We have not taken the time to dig and figure out what is the source of the voice of fear in our lives. Did something happen to us in our childhoods that we processed through a childlike lens? And have we not taken the time to reassess that situation? Consider what the scripture says regarding fear:

> *For God hath not given us the spirit of fear; but of power, and of love, and of a sound mind.*
>
> *~2 Timothy 1:7*

God never intended for us to have a spirit of fear. This does not mean that we will not be afraid at times There was just never an intention for us to walk in the spirit of fear. His desire for us was not to come into agreement with any spirit other than His. How do we have a spirit of fear? We allow our minds to come into agreement with a thought or an image. Therefore, 2 Corinthians 10:5 tells us to cast down every imagination and every high thing that exalts itself against the knowledge of Jesus Christ. So, we do not allow these thoughts or images to take up space in our minds.

> *But now thus saith the Lord that created thee, O Jacob, and he that formed thee, O Israel, Fear not: for I have redeemed*

thee, I have called thee by thy name; thou art mine.

~Isaiah 43:1

The Lord knew us before we were born; in fact, He formed us. So, He is not caught off guard by our situations. Consequently, He tells us to not fear and to not allow fear to take us off course or out of alignment with His plan for our lives. For God has already paid the price for the disappointments we have and will experience, and He has already paid for our freedom. He has called us, named us, and claimed us. For we are his workmanship, created in Christ Jesus unto good works, which God hath before ordained that we should walk in them (*Ephesians 2:10*).

And the Lord, he it is that doth go before thee; he will be with thee, he will not fail thee, neither forsake thee: fear not, neither be dismayed.

~Deuteronomy 31:8

Again, God tells us to fear not, because He has gone before us. The part I personally enjoy is, He will not fail us. Most of our fears come from some level or layer of disappointment. Someone or something we once had complete trust in let us down, and that has become a place for fear to grow. The good news is that God has gone before us, He knows the end, but stands at the beginning. There is no need to fear or to feel unsettled because He will not leave us.

> *There is no fear in love; but perfect love casteth out fear: because fear hath torment. He that feareth is not made perfect in love.*
>
> *~I John 4:18*

This verse is one of my personal favorites. Wherever love exists, there is no fear, because the opposite of fear is faith. When faith is present, there is complete trust and fear cannot exist. What does the Bible mean when it says that perfect love casts out fear? The word "perfect" here means complete or full, not lacking in anything. If we accept the love of Christ, we will not be afraid. On the contrary, if we are afraid, we are missing something in our understanding of the love of Jesus.

> *And we know that all things work together for good to them that love God, to them who are the called according to his purpose.*
>
> *~Roman 8:28*

One way to guard our hearts against fear is to hide this verse deep in our hearts. Understand that regardless of what is happening in the physical, there is no need to worry because Romans 8:28 discusses the destiny of every situation. AND we know that ALL things work together for the good of them that love the Lord and who are called to His purpose.

The year 2020 seemed like an unusual year. Although previous generations had endured challenging times and many nations in the world have lived through wars, poor leadership, and bad systems, there was a global pandemic making its rounds in the Earth (well technically, this is still going on while I am writing). Coronavirus (COVID-19) spread across several countries and affected everyone in some capacity. First, the news mentioned that there was a virus spreading around China. Most of us did not really understand how the initial communication about the virus would impact our lives. What's amazing is, we've experienced the craziness of EBOLA when it was spreading, but somehow that disease had been contained, even though the disease came to the USA. Then COVID-19 came to our country, and eventually to our individual states, and then it showed up in our cities or towns.

Since the arrival of COVID-19, the world has repeatedly shut down from normal operations. Safer at-home restrictions were put in place everywhere. Schools were closed, and most employers found a way to allow their employees to work from home. But there were those who were considered essential workers, such as grocery store workers, healthcare manufacturers, along with those working in the areas of food, agriculture, corrections, and many other fields. We should take a moment and thank those who continued to work outside of their homes during the pandemic. (Note: if that's you, thank you for your service.)

Many people lost their jobs because many nonessential businesses needed to shut down. Food service was shifted to drive-thru, curbside, and take-out orders only. A great number of businesses were shut down indefinitely. In-person church services were canceled in some parts of the world. Of course, we understand that there are challenges in worship during a pandemic, but many of us had never experienced not being able to gather to worship. The only other disaster I can ever recall closing the church building were snowstorms.

After dealing with all these sudden changes, we were not able to see loved ones for a long period of time. Many of us lost loved ones at a time when we could not even be with them as they transitioned from this world. Our ability to visit our loved ones in the hospital was taken away from us, and our only communication with them was through a scheduled video call.

In April of last year, I lost my grandmother. My grandmother had been diagnosed with COVID-19, and to make matters worse, she had pre-existing conditions. I recall having Zoom calls with the family to talk with her during her time in the hospital. She beat COVID-19 and was able to leave the hospital, but COVID worsened her pre-existing conditions. Shortly after her release from the hospital, she departed from the Earth. Our last time with her was spent on video chat, and we attended her home-going service via live video streaming. There may come a time when connecting with people and attending events virtually may be considered normal, but this was a first for us, and it made it even more painful.

The pandemic outbreak period was a time that many of us spent in the fetal position, not just individually, but collectively. The world was in a fetal position with their backs against the wall, confused about how to move forward or if there was even going to be a future. Fear was a big driver for most of the world, including believers. The media played a huge role in the way information was disseminated. Many media stations reported on the pandemic in a way that seemed as if the world was ending. On top of the news, there was so much misinformation spread throughout social media and sometimes through the news media outlets. People feared running out of toilet paper, causing many to run to the store and stockpile their houses with toilet paper and other necessities.

The pandemic was a collective trauma that we all faced together. At times, it can all still feel so unbearable. Time stopped, and we were forced to really pay attention to some of the major issues that still exist in this world today. While there had been many police brutality situations in times past, we were forced to sit and watch George Floyd be murdered by police because of the pandemic.

During the pandemic, fear was the dominant energy in the atmosphere. Families were afraid of the unknown, uncertainty and the future. Another contributor to all this uncertainty was the incredible faith the world placed in science and on the scientist. For centuries, we relied on science to inform us and to be ahead of the current climate of the world. However, most of the science on the virus was unclear or being discovered in real-time. Decision-makers were forced to make calls regarding research that was still new and barely tested. Frontline healthcare workers were not sure how to treat or develop tests for the virus. Lack of preparation and follow-through led research teams to fall behind in their fight against COVID.

The principle here is that lack of preparation is a breeding ground for fear. Whenever or wherever you are unprepared and unknowledgeable, fear can easily creep into that space. God said, "My people perish for the lack of knowledge." What He's saying in this scripture is, wherever we are not knowledgeable, there will be room for other voices to exist.

The Lord is our Encourager, so when we feel overwhelmed by everything or too caught up in the cares of this life, we can lean on Christ, our Savior, for He is indeed the lifter of our heads. He brings us up beyond the level we are on and establishes us in His ways.

God is so faithful that no matter how much you try to walk in fear, there is a lesson coming that will teach you the strategy of faith.
Make this declaration with me: I will not submit to the spirit of fear, and even though some ungodly thoughts may exist in my head, I am no longer a slave to those mindsets of fear.

But thou, O LORD, art a shield for me; my glory, and the lifter up of my head.

~Psalms 3:3

Chapter 4

(The Doubts)

Around age twenty-four, I was close to completing my first Master's degree. I decided to give my car to my little sister, so I was in the market to purchase my first car from the car lot. I was super nervous about starting this process because of the stories I'd heard from adults and the challenges I saw my parents face while at the dealership. There was this perceived notion that all car salesmen were shady and could not be trusted. I believed that every dealership would charge me more money than I could afford and push me into a purchase I did not want.

I recall finding all the adults I knew who had been somewhat successful at the local car dealerships, and I asked them for wisdom. I learned several tactics, like not giving the salesperson any indication of the type of car you want and not showing any excitement, in addition to being okay with walking away without a car and knowing how to be firm on your offer.

With all this advice in mind, I went to my first car dealership to purchase a car. I ended up at a Hyundai dealership, and while there, I identified the Hyundai Sonata as an affordable car. All the same, my previous car had been a 2004 Hyundai Sonata. I spoke with the car salesman, and we agreed on a 2011 used Hyundai Sonata at a certain price. I put one hundred dollars down on the car and said I would be back with my dad so he could check the car out. Well, I came back that week and the car salesmen had already sold the car to someone else. He then made me a promise that he would sell me a brand new 2012 Sonata with zero miles on the car for the same price as the other car we'd originally agreed upon. I was very skeptical of this offer. Why would the car salesman want to favor me in such a way that he would be willing to sell me a better car for the same price? I thought there was supposed to be a fight, a war between the salesman and my will. I was absolutely convinced that I had to prove that I wasn't gullible because of all the car buying stories I'd heard.

What I did not process was the Word of God and what He had given me access to. I had all the intellectual knowledge of the car buying process with the tactics and strategies. What I did not have, however, was the Word of God hidden in my heart so I could move past the place of doubt I was in and into the place of trust. I don't mean that I needed to put my trust in the car salesperson, but I needed to put my trust in my God, knowing that favor was with me regardless of how many strategies I'd learned.

I let doubt paralyze me and keep me out of what God was trying to do in my life. I did not go back to the dealership until thirty days later. I was able to purchase my first car at a significant discount with only one thousand dollars down and a low interest rate.

From this moment on, I became totally confident in the process and the spirit of doubt was lifted off my mind regarding the car buying process. After this, I went car shopping with friends on a few occasions; I was their emotional support and I helped them negotiate the best deals. I had moved into a new mindset. I now knew without a shadow of a doubt that we would leave the dealership in the best cars. I had this mindset because I knew God was with us.

Recently, my husband decided that he wanted a luxury car. This brought me back to a place of doubt. Up until that point, the cars we'd purchased and the cars our friends had purchased had been doable. By this, I mean the cars came with long-term warranties or normal repairs would be inexpensive. Purchasing a luxury car, on the other hand, took much more research and intentionality to get the best offer. A luxury car purchase meant warranties are short-lived and normal repairs would be much more costly. After purchasing the car, we would have to think about maintenance, brakes, and tires. All of these came to mind, instead of positive thoughts. Doubt was running rampant in my mind.

We spent just about two years coming up with an agreement regarding the type of car we'd buy and the best dealership to purchase the car from. We traveled to every dealership we could to test drive cars and discuss the prices of the vehicles. I spent a good seven months of this process pregnant. Sometimes, we would walk the lots, and at other times, the salesperson would drive us around. We test drove every third row SUV there was on the market. After all this research and testing, we still couldn't come to an agreement regarding a car.

Eventually, we ended up buying a car that we could both agree on. What made this decision easier for me was the moment we ended up taking a trip in the car we would end up buying. I believe the ride in the car helped me to deal with the doubt that was lingering in my mind. I realize now that the reason this process took so long is because I was once again having issues with uncertainty and disbelief. Buying a luxury car came with more responsibility than buying a standard vehicle. For some reason, I had doubts regarding our ability to take care of that level of responsibility. When the right amount of pressure is applied, everything that is lying dormant or deep inside of you will come out of you. So, while doubt may have been dealt with when buying an affordable Hyundai, doubt was revealed when the time had come to purchase a higher-level car. I knew that we could afford the car, but I feared the unknown.

Doubt is a feeling of uncertainty or lack of conviction, according to Oxford Languages dictionary. The verb doubt means to disbelieve a person at their word or question the truth or a fact. How many times does God speak to us concerning a thing, and we say that we believe Him, even though some level of doubt exists in our minds? If we are not careful, our first thought may be belief, but the second thought could potentially be blatant doubt regarding

God and His Word. Doubt will disguise itself as an angel of light, causing us to miss out on the manifestation of the promise. A simple comment from a friend questioning if we're ready or not could give way to doubt. Doubt can be defined as the uncertainties that exist in our minds, and of course, these uncertainties can become debilitating. Oftentimes, people mistake doubt for fear, thinking that they are just afraid of what is to come, but in reality, they do not completely trust God.

There is a significant difference between doubt and fear. Fear is an emotion caused by a perceived danger. Doubt is the need to question a person or event; it is a feeling of uncertainty. Doubt is questioning whether the process would work, but fear is the emotions we experience while in the process. The key difference here is that you can feel the fear and do it anyway, but with doubt, there is really no ability to move forward. When doubt is present, we feel the need to question everything because there is some level of mistrust in the person, process, or system. There will be a need to work through the doubt. So much can happen when dealing with doubt; we can delay, deny, or disqualify ourselves from the promises God intended for our lives. For example, God may have spoken a word concerning a certain job, car, house, or even a spouse, but because we live with doubt in our minds, we will count ourselves out of what God is trying to do in our lives as believers.

For many of us, our first thought is filled with faith; we believe that God is going to do some crazy things in our lives. Our second or third thoughts are filled with doubt. We reason, "Why would God do something great in my life? He should choose someone else." To break this vicious cycle, the important thing to do is to deal with any thoughts of doubt that may come. Never allow them to linger. The Bible often speaks of people who have doubt or unbelief, and how nothing can get accomplished through them.

The challenge with doubt in our hearts is that there is a real difficulty in seeing the actual promises of God in our lives because with doubt, we do not have total belief. Let's look at the passage of scripture below:

> *But whoever has doubts is condemned if he eats, because the eating is not from faith. For whatever does not proceed from faith is sin.*
>
> *~Romans 14:23*

Wow, the KJV gives everything straight. If what we are doing is not done in faith, our action itself is sin. I know we always look at sin as some action that dishonors God. Sin has much more to do with the posture or position of our hearts than it has to do with our actions. What is truly in our hearts regarding what God has spoken to us? If our actions do not align with our belief systems, we are in sin. For example, we were asked to wash the dishes when we were children. We did as we were told, but the posture of our hearts doubted the importance of this action. The heart posture can devalue the purpose behind the action, causing us to lose the wisdom behind the action.

But when you ask, you must believe and not doubt, because the one who doubts is like a wave of the sea, blown and tossed by the wind.

~James 1:6

When we have doubts, we can be thrown around by every wind of doctrine. Doubts can bring instability to our belief systems. This confusion makes it difficult for us to remain anchored. For example, have you ever met a person who was Christian one day, but by next week, that person is Muslim, and the week after that, he or she is Buddhist? This happens when there are some doubts that have not been addressed. These doubts created access to the enemy, allowing the whispers of the wind to creep into their minds.

And Jesus answered them, "Truly, I say to you, if you have faith and do not doubt, you will not only do what has been done to the fig tree, but even if you say to this mountain, 'Be taken up and thrown into the sea,' it will happen."

~Matthew 21:21

The ability to have faith and not doubt God empowers us to be able to do the works that Jesus did and more. If we can have complete trust in God, we are able to speak things into existence. There is power in being able to silence the thoughts that are not needed in our minds and to dwell on the thoughts that matter. Let our minds think on these things, the things that Jesus directed us to think on. Oftentimes, people compare our minds to a train station; many thoughts come through like trains. We must decide which trains we will ride. Chose the thoughts that will lead to faith!

Our case study for doubt is Abraham. Abraham had a history with God. God had given him direction to leave his country, his father's house and to follow Him into an unknown land. Abraham followed the voice of God without hesitation. Except for the promise of a son, Abraham believed God.

Abraham had come from a family of idol worshipers. Idol worshipers during this time would basically create physical objects that they would worship. For them, there was power in being able to worship something they could see. Also, idol worshipers would become enamored by the created thing and lose sight of the actual Creator.

God made Abram several promises before he became Abraham. The most challenging one for Abram to believe wholeheartedly was the one that defied normality. This was the promise that God would make Abram a great nation; this is because Abram left his father's house when he was seventy-five years old. With no children, how could God make him a great nation? At the age of seventy-five, how could Abram even produce any children? This is something that was considered physically possible. Take a look at the text below:

> *Now the Lord had said unto Abram, Get thee out of thy country, and from thy kindred, and from thy father's house, unto a land that I will shew thee:*

And I will make of thee a great nation, and I will bless thee, and make thy name great; and thou shalt be a blessing: And I will bless them that bless thee and curse him that curseth thee: and in thee shall all families of the earth be blessed. So Abram departed, as the Lord had spoken unto him; and Lot went with him: and Abram was seventy and five years old when he departed out of Haran. And Abram took Sarai his wife, and Lot his brother's son, and all their substance that they had gathered, and the souls that they had gotten in Haran; and they went forth to go into the land of Canaan; and into the land of Canaan they came. And Abram passed through the land unto the place of Sichem, unto the plain of Moreh. And the Canaanite was then in the land. And the Lord appeared unto Abram, and said, Unto thy seed will I give this land: and there builded he an altar unto the Lord, who appeared unto him.

~Genesis 12:1-7

How many of us get a word from God that He has called us out of a place of familiarity and into unknown territory? In this unknown place, God is looking for us to produce something that seems physically, mentally, and emotionally impossible. Make this confession with me right now: Lord, I believe, but help any place of unbelief in me. I command those untapped areas of my mind to come into alignment with Your will for my life!

In the seasons between the promise and the manifestation, one of the main mind battles to overcome is doubt. The spirit of doubt makes many attempts to get us to believe something contrary to what God has spoken over us. The spirit of doubt will try to get to us through our circle of friends, our family members and even through our spouses. It is important to remain steadfast regarding what God has spoken to us and to commit those declarations to our hearts.

One of the ways the spirit of doubt will try to attack us is to get us to settle on something close to the promise, but not precisely the promise. For example, let's say that God spoke to you concerning a certain house that you were going to buy. He gave you specific details regarding the location and what the interior of the house would be like. One day, you find a house that is the right location, but the details don't match the description of the house that God gave you. You decide to go ahead with purchasing the house because the house seems close enough to what God said. Well, that exposes the spirit of doubt in your heart. For whatever reason, there is a small space of doubt in your heart that is keeping you from God's best.

Many times, uncertainty comes in the season when there is space and time in between the spoken Word of God and the manifestation of God's promise. Genesis 8:22 says, "While the earth remaineth, seedtime and harvest, and cold and heat, and summer and winter, and day and night shall not cease." There is a season of time between sowing and the actual harvest. We can also call this space of time a waiting period.

The distance between the Word of the Lord and the manifestation of that Word is where most people get lost. We get extremely excited when we hear the Word, but the difficulty is during the waiting period. The space in-between time is where we lose our hope, desires, and passion.

Abram was in a similar situation. There was a promise made to him, but he had some doubts. He was seventy-five years old and just beginning his journey with the Lord in uncharted territory. Most of the things the Lord spoke to him seemed attainable, but becoming a great nation looked nearly impossible. Time had passed, and there didn't seem to be any initiative being taken by God towards what He had spoken. So, Sarai, Abram's wife, gave Abram her maidservant, Hagar. Hagar was able to get pregnant and bring a son into the world with no issues. Sarai suddenly became jealous of the woman she'd chosen to give to her husband. Eventually, Sarai asked for Abram to evict Hagar from their home and their lives, because she could not deal with the fact that Hagar had been able to get pregnant. God's Word that He would make Abram a great nation was to come to pass through his son, Isaac, but Abram and Sarai's doubt provoked them to set the stage for Ishmael's arrival instead. Just a small amount of doubt will keep us out of the promises of God and have us settling for something less than God's best. Look at the verses below to see more about Sarai and Abram, and how they used Hagar:

> *Now Sarai Abram's wife bare him no children: and she had an handmaid, an Egyptian, whose name was Hagar. And Sarai said unto Abram, Behold now, the Lord hath restrained me from bearing: I pray thee, go in unto my maid; it may be that I may obtain children by her. And Abram hearkened to the voice of Sarai. And Sarai Abram's wife took Hagar her maid the Egyptian, after Abram had dwelt ten years in the land of Canaan, and gave her to her husband*

Abram to be his wife. And he went in unto Hagar, and she conceived: and when she saw that she had conceived, her mistress was despised in her eyes. And Sarai said unto Abram, My wrong be upon thee: I have given my maid into thy bosom; and when she saw that she had conceived, I was despised in her eyes: the Lord judge between me and thee. But Abram said unto Sarai, Behold, thy maid is in thine hand; do to her as it pleaseth thee. And when Sarai dealt hardly with her, she fled from her face. And the angel of the Lord found her by a fountain of water in the wilderness, by the fountain in the way to Shur. And he said, Hagar, Sarai's maid, whence camest thou? and whither wilt thou go? And she said, I flee from the face of my mistress Sarai. And the angel of the Lord said unto her, Return to thy mistress, and submit thyself under her hands. And the angel of the Lord said unto her, I will multiply thy seed exceedingly, that it shall not be numbered for multitude. And the angel of the Lord said unto her, Behold, thou art with child and shalt bear a son, and shalt call his name Ishmael; because the Lord hath heard thy affliction. And he will be a wild man; his hand will be against every man, and every man's hand against him; and he shall dwell in the presence of all his brethren. And she called the name of the Lord that spake unto her, Thou God seest me: for she said, Have I also here looked after him that seeth me? Wherefore the well was called Beerlahairoi; behold, it is between Kadesh and Bered. And Hagar bare Abram a son: and Abram called his son's name, which Hagar bare, Ishmael. And Abram was fourscore and six years old, when Hagar bare Ishmael to Abram.

~Genesis 16:1-16

At age 86, Abram birthed his first child by Hagar, his wife's maidservant. This was not the promise that was to come through Sarai.

Their uncertainty about the promise led them astray and provoked them to take matters into their own hands. I can envision Abram and Sarai considering the odds that had been stacked against them, including their ages and their many failed attempts to get pregnant. When we focus on our failures and our own limitations, we take our eyes off God. Please know that if He said it, it will happen. Many of us will try to hold on to things much longer than we should. Consequently, we try to piece things together because we think God needs our assistance in the matter. However, He knew us before any of this. He knew us when we were in the dark, and He STILL knows us now that we are in His marvelous light.

The interesting part about the story is the moment when Abraham laughed at God after God reminded him of the covenant they'd made. When I first read this, I will admit, I thought that Abraham and Sarah were laughing at God because they did not believe His promise. Later, I realized in my own journey that I have experienced this type of laughter. I think about the moment when you know God said something would happen, but so much time has gone by that the promise no longer seems like a good fit. But if God said it, regardless of what science, people, or the media says, the promise still stands.

Let's go back to my car buying experience and all the doubt that existed throughout that process. When the time came to purchase a luxury car, my husband and I laughed in that moment. We had given up on the process because we could not agree on a vehicle. My husband has this great faith; he is always ready to walk on water in every situation, but I am more of a practical person. I like to figure out how to make the faith moves fit in our lives. So, when the time came to make the purchase, I laughed because I'd never imagined that we would be driving the car at this point in life. Nevertheless, I have always imagined this for us. I could only trust what I could physically see, so I placed certain events further down the road for us. There were blessings that I had not accounted for that were being set in place for us.

We also laugh when we realize that God is still mindful of us. He has not forgotten about us. He is with us, and He knows more than we know. There is a key piece in the scripture that we often miss. Abraham fell to his face before laughing. We cannot ignore this scripture, because it denotes a level of submission on his part and the fact that he understood that God is God. His thoughts are greater than our thoughts and bigger than we could have ever ask or imagine. Look at the verses below to see more about the covenant being revisited:

> *And when Abram was ninety years old and nine, the Lord appeared to Abram, and said unto him, I am the Almighty God; walk before me, and be thou perfect. And I will make my covenant between me and thee, and will multiply thee exceedingly. And Abram fell on his face: and God talked with him, saying, As for me, behold, my covenant is with thee, and thou shalt be a father of many*

nations. Neither shall thy name any more be called Abram, but thy name shall be Abraham; for a father of many nations have I made thee. And I will make thee exceeding fruitful, and I will make nations of thee, and kings shall come out of thee. And I will establish my covenant between me and thee and thy seed after thee in their generations for an everlasting covenant, to be a God unto thee, and to thy seed after thee. And I will give unto thee, and to thy seed after thee, the land wherein thou art a stranger, all the land of Canaan, for an everlasting possession; and I will be their God. And God said unto Abraham, Thou shalt keep my covenant therefore, thou, and thy seed after thee in their generations. This is my covenant, which ye shall keep, between me and you and thy seed after thee; Every man child among you shall be circumcised. And ye shall circumcise the flesh of your foreskin; and it shall be a token of the covenant betwixt me and you. And he that is eight days old shall be circumcised among you, every man child in your generations, he that is born in the house, or bought with money of any stranger, which is not of thy seed. He that is born in thy house, and he that is bought with thy money, must needs be circumcised: and my covenant shall be in your flesh for an everlasting covenant. And the uncircumcised man child whose flesh of his foreskin is not circumcised, that soul shall be cut off from his people; he hath broken my covenant. And God said unto Abraham, As for Sarai thy wife, thou shalt not call her name Sarai, but Sarah shall her name be. And I will bless her, and give thee a son also of her: yea, I will bless her, and she shall be a mother of nations; kings of people shall be of her. Then Abraham fell upon his face, and laughed, and said in his heart, Shall a child be born unto him that is an hundred years old? and shall Sarah, that is ninety years old, bear? And

Abraham said unto God, O that Ishmael might live before thee! And God said, Sarah thy wife shall bear thee a son indeed; and thou shalt call his name Isaac: and I will establish my covenant with him for an everlasting covenant, and with his seed after him. And as for Ishmael, I have heard thee: Behold, I have blessed him, and will make him fruitful, and will multiply him exceedingly; twelve princes shall he beget, and I will make him a great nation. But my covenant will I establish with Isaac, which Sarah shall bear unto thee at this set time in the next year.

~Genesis 17:1- 21

We cannot allow the low "pre-designed places" to keep us outside of faith. The low places were intended for us to grow our faith. I believe when Abraham fell to his face, his faith grew. He graduated from faith to the next level of hope. He moved from just learning to trust God to knowing that God was going to give them a child.

If you are in a low season, understand that this season was not meant to harm you. In Jeremiah 29:11, God said, "For I know the thoughts that I think toward you, saith the LORD, thoughts of peace, and not of evil, to give you an expected end." These seasons were meant to bring us into a great expected end and to prosper us. Part of prospering us is increasing our faith. When our faith grows, our level of response increases. We can avoid certain pitfalls that would keep us down for days, months or even years. Full grown faith can respond to seasons by zooming in on the promises of God and zooming out on the obstacles surrounding those promises. We can zoom out of our emotions and zoom in on the Word of God to allow the Holy Spirit to speak to us concerning the bigger picture.

I believe that even in reading this book, our faith is being stirred and encouraged. The Lord is saying, "Get up from that fetal position or that pit, and stand up in full confidence, knowing that I am your God! You are what I was looking for this entire time—your submission, your faith, your love. I am the God who heals you and brings you to the place of faith." Take a moment here to reflect on the seasons of difficulty in your life and give those places over to the Lord. Allow Him to position and posture your heart so that you will know that God is with you and has been with you the entire time.

Be encouraged by the passage of scripture below, which lets us see the promise come to pass!

> *And the Lord visited Sarah as he had said, and the Lord did unto Sarah as he had spoken. For Sarah conceived, and bare Abraham a son in his old age, at the set time of which God had spoken to him. And Abraham called the name of his son that was born unto him, whom Sarah bare to him, Isaac. And Abraham circumcised his son Isaac being eight days old, as God had commanded him. And Abraham was an hundred years old, when his son Isaac was born unto*

him. And Sarah said, God hath made me to laugh, so that all that hear will laugh with me. And she said, Who would have said unto Abraham, that Sarah should have given children suck? for I have born him a son in his old age.

~Genesis 21:1-7

For Abraham and Sarah had a son named Isaac at the set time in which God told them. Is that God's way of saying, "I told you I would do it, didn't I?" Basically, God was letting them know that He had them the whole time. He'd never left them. He was more committed to the promise than they were!

After Abraham got up from his falling on his face and laughing with God, he made sure to obey God immediately. God gave him instructions to circumcise every man child. Abraham made sure to circumcise everyone, including Isaac. When faith grows, obedience becomes easier.

From the story of Abraham, Sarah, and Isaac, there are ten ways doubt tries to enter our hearts in our journeys.

1. **Different than expectation** – God gives us a word concerning our lives, our journeys, or what is to come. We almost immediately begin to plan out what that looks like in our lives. For example, God says we are going to get a degree. We decide that this means that right after college, we are going straight to grad school to complete our degrees. What if God meant that He would give us the degrees after we'd worked for a few years? God may want to address some character issues that He wants to work into us and out of us before we go to college. Be encouraged by Colossians 3:2, which says, "Set your affection on things above, not on things on the earth."
2. **Worth the wait**- "Patience is a virtue I desire." This is one of the lines in an

old song. The space of time that we find ourselves waiting for something often serves as a breeding ground for doubt, whether we are waiting for food, pregnancy, or someone to come. There is almost always some thought of uncertainty that tries to creep into our minds. James 1:4 reads, “But let patience have her perfect work, that ye may be perfect and entire, wanting nothing.”

3. **Timing is everything**- Again, we always have our lives on this linear scale. First comes the degree, then comes marriage. After marriage comes the house, followed by a baby. God does not fit into the American dream or some linear process. God is much bigger than what we think. Proverbs 16:3 states, “Commit thy works unto the LORD, and thy thoughts shall be established.” Make this declaration with me from Psalms 31:5. “My times are in thy hand: deliver me from the hand of mine

enemies, and from them that persecute me. My times, time, and timing are in the hands of the Lord."

4. **Character over inconvenience** – The Lord is concerned with our character over our convenience. Oftentimes, we tell ourselves that if God would just give us the promises minus all the transitions, grief, and pain, we would be better off. However, God is looking for certain character traits to be represented in our lives.
5. **Excitement fades**- During our journeys, there will be moments when excitement fades. This happens when we are tired of waiting, enduring, and hoping for everything that God promised us. Nehemiah gives us an excellent example to follow, in that he reminds us that the joy of the Lord is our strength. Be strengthened in recalling to yourself the very joy that brought you to the path you are on with Christ. Nehemiah 8:10 reads,

"Then he said unto them, Go your way, eat the fat, and drink the sweet, and send portions unto them for whom nothing is prepared: for this day is holy unto our LORD: neither be ye sorry; for the joy of the LORD is your strength."

6. **Management Difficult** – Sometimes, the timing of God can feel like the most difficult season; for example, having a baby later in life. How exactly are we going to manage this promise? Why not give us what we want at the time that is most optimal in our eyes?
7. **Lose hope**- In the process of waiting, we oftentimes lose sight of the promise and begin to grow weary. Proverbs 13:12 says, "Hope deferred maketh the heart sick: but when the desire cometh, it is a tree of life." So, during these times, we must make sure we are utilizing Jude 1:20, which reads, "But ye, beloved, building up

yourselves on your most holy faith, praying in the Holy Ghost."

8. **Easier roads available** – There was a simple way to make sure that Abraham had a child before he died. This way, they could ensure that God's promise was honored by making Abraham's seed a great nation. Philippians 4:6-7 reads, "Be careful for nothing; but in everything by prayer and supplication with thanksgiving let your requests be made known unto God. And the peace of God, which passeth all understanding, shall keep your hearts and minds through Christ Jesus."
9. **Competition** – At church, we often hear our pastors say, "Look to your left and look to your right." During the journey of life, it is important that we do not look to our lefts or our rights, but we must remain focused on our paths and what God has called us to. I am a runner. In all the races I have run, I have learned that each runner

must run their own race. This verse would encourage me anytime I found myself running my own race. 1 Corinthians 9:24 says, "Know ye not that they which run in a race run all, but one receiveth the prize? So run, that ye may obtain."

10. **Keep Mind Fixed** – What better way to avoid doubt than to keep your mind on Jesus, as the old folks would say? Isaiah 26:3 reads, "Thou wilt keep him in perfect peace, whose mind is is stayed on thee: because he trusteth in thee."

Overall, just remember this—if God said it, then believe God because whatever He said is coming to pass. Despite what is going on in our lives right now, whatever pit we may find ourselves in, we must continue to look up, after all, we are alive, so we have a reason to give God glory.

It is of the Lord's mercies that we are not consumed, because his compassions fail not. They are new every morning: great is thy faithfulness.

~Lamentations 3:22

Chapter 5

(Insecurity)

Life has a way of getting us into a fetal position through the many different paths we find ourselves on, including grief, pain, or transition. Sometimes, the chaos of daily life will propel us into the low places.

Instead of looking for someone else to be the rock for us, there is a common understanding amongst believers that Jesus has already done the work for us, which means that we do not have to wait on a mediator. This does not negate the fact that there are systematic issues in the world. As followers of Christ, we are in the world but not of the world. So, our lives should be lived on a level that is pleasing to the Father. It is important that we understand the work, prayer, and relationship we need to move forward will only come through us. When we understand this and realize no one is coming to do the work for us, the process becomes easier.

Despite the fears we may feel and the doubts we may entertain, we must accept the work of Jesus Christ in our lives; this way, we can continue our journeys in peace. Peace in our journeys comes when we have reconciled our relationships with Jesus Christ and when we fully recognize His finished work on the cross. In the chapters to come, we will discuss more about what Jesus has done to free us from the low places.

So far, we have been discussing the fetal position or the low place because of trauma or something challenging that happened to us. But what happens when the Word of the Lord sends you to the fetal position? What happens when the instructions you receive from God send you into the low place? Do you remember Jonah? He got instructions, and somehow ended up in the ultimate low place: the belly of the whale.

In this chapter, we will look at insecurity. Our insecurities are oftentimes the result of a voice in our heads that keeps us bound and not in the will of God. There are two biblical characters we want to investigate as our case studies. They are Gideon and Nehemiah. Gideon, of course, represents an insecure leader, and Nehemiah represents a confident leader. Consider the passages of scripture below to learn more about Gideon. Lastly, we will contrast the two biblical leaders.

Background of Gideon:

> *And the children of Israel did evil in the sight of the Lord: and the Lord delivered them into the hand of Midian seven years. And the hand of Midian prevailed against Israel: and because of the Midianites the children of Israel made them the dens which are in the mountains, and caves, and strong holds. And so it was, when Israel had sown, that the Midianites came up, and the Amalekites, and the children of the east, even they came up against them;*

And they encamped against them, and destroyed the increase of the earth, till thou come unto Gaza, and left no sustenance for Israel, neither sheep, nor ox, nor ass. For they came up with their cattle and their tents, and they came as grasshoppers for multitude; for both they and their camels were without number: and they entered into the land to destroy it. And Israel was greatly impoverished because of the Midianites; and the children of Israel cried unto the Lord.

~Judges 6:1-6

Gideon was from the tribe of Manasseh, which was a part of the children of Israel. The children of Israel had been dominated by the Midianites for seven years. The children of Israel would hide out in caves, and anything the children of Israel planted, would be taken. The Midianites basically put the children of Israel in poverty. So, the children of Israel cried out to the Lord for help. Because of their disobedience, the Lord sent a famine in their land by using the Midianites. Take a closer look at the Lord's response to their call for help in the verses below:

> *And it came to pass, when the children of Israel cried unto the Lord because of the Midianites, That the Lord sent a prophet unto the children of Israel, which said unto them, Thus saith the Lord God of Israel, I brought you up from Egypt, and brought you forth out of the house of bondage; And I delivered you out of the hand of the Egyptians, and out of the hand of all that oppressed you, and drave them out from before you, and gave you their land; And I said unto you, I am the Lord your God; fear not the gods of the Amorites, in whose land ye dwell: but ye have not obeyed my voice.*
>
> *~Judges 6:7-10*

The Lord sent the children of Israel a prophet to remind them of what He had already done for them. The Lord brought them out of Egypt and out of the oppression, reminding the children of Israel to not fear the Midianites. But the Lord also recognized their disobedience. So, the Lord acknowledged the fact that Israel was following other voices, and not His voice. Israel made a choice in their journey to listen to other voices, rather than God's voice. How many times in our journeys have we gotten so caught up in the trip that we've missed God's voice? The Lord may have just delivered us out of a problematic relationship and brought us into a new land. However, somehow along the way, we lost sight of His voice and began to be directed by other voices, like the voice of insecurity. Let us look at the next few verses to see God's plan to still deliver the children of Israel, even though they had gone astray.

Gideon's Insecurity

> *And there came an angel of the Lord, and sat under an oak which was in Ophrah, that pertained unto Joash the Abiezrite: and his son Gideon threshed wheat by the winepress, to hide it from the Midianites. And the angel of the Lord appeared unto him, and said*

unto him, The Lord is with thee, thou mighty man of valour. And Gideon said unto him, Oh my Lord, if the Lord be with us, why then is all this befallen us? And where be all his miracles which our fathers told us of, saying, Did not the Lord bring us up from Egypt? But now the Lord hath forsaken us, and delivered us into the hands of the Midianites. And the Lord looked upon him, and said, Go in this thy might, and thou shalt save Israel from the hand of the Midianites: have not I sent thee? And he said unto him, Oh my Lord, wherewith shall I save Israel? Behold, my family is poor in Manasseh, and I am the least in my father's house.
And the Lord said unto him, Surely I will be with thee, and thou shalt smite the Midianites as one man.

~Judges 6:11-16

The Lord approached Gideon, letting him know that He was with him. Gideon questioned the Lord this way. He said (paraphrased), “If you are with us, why has all of this happened?” Gideon wondered if this God could be the same God that folks had testified about, and if so, why had He turned them over to Midian? The Lord gave Gideon the strength to be the sent one, and He questioned Gideon about his authority. Gideon then allowed the voice of insecurity to become more pronounced in his mind. “Why me, Lord?” Gideon questioned how he could save Israel, after all, he was from the weakest tribe, which was Manasseh. This tribe was basically considered the bottom of the barrel amongst other tribes. How could God use Gideon?

God asked Gideon to believe in Him. He told him that He would be with him, and that Israel would defeat Midian. We see here that the Word of the Lord put pressure on Gideon. This uncovered the voice of insecurity that had been dormant in Gideon's heart. The instructions from the Lord sent Gideon to a low place. He thought to himself, “Who am I to go and save the children of Israel?” The Lord was asking Gideon to come out of the posture of insecurity and step into his rightful place as an intercessor for God's people.

This means that the fetal position was also meant to bring us into a place of intercession, provoking us to fight for our families, cities, nations, and our planet. We will address this more in detail later, but let us continue to investigate Gideon's story.

> *And it came to pass the same night, that the Lord said unto him, Take thy father's young bullock, even the second bullock of seven years old, and throw down the altar of Baal that thy father hath, and cut down the grove that is by it: And build an altar unto the Lord thy God upon the top of this rock, in the ordered place, and take the second bullock, and offer a burnt sacrifice with the wood of the grove which thou shalt cut down.*
> *Then Gideon took ten men of his servants, and did as the Lord had said unto him: and so it was, because he feared his father's household, and the*

men of the city, that he could not do it by day, that he did it by night.

~Judges 6:25- 27

The Lord told Gideon to tear down the altars that had been lifted to other gods, and to raise an altar up to Him. Gideon did what the Lord told him, but he was afraid of the men of the city and his father's household, so he did everything at night. Now, the interesting point here is that when the angel of the Lord approached Gideon, hc called him a mighty man of valor. He was basically saying that Gideon was a great warrior, but this brings to question—if he was a great warrior, why was he doing what God told him to do at night while afraid? What ungodly report did Gideon believe about himself? What had Gideon come into agreement with that had never been intended for his life? I bet by now, you have guessed it—the voice of insecurity.

The voice of insecurity caused him to forget what God said and to call himself something else. Insecurity gave him a negative self-image, causing him to become timid and afraid, when God called him a mighty warrior. This is like many of us. We hear the Word of the Lord and His instructions; that's when we suddenly find ourselves in a pit. “The journey from prophecy to fulfillment takes faith, hope and love” (Source: Apostle Bryan Meadows). You need:

1. Faith toward God, yourself, and others.
2. Hope. This is believing that the promise will come to pass.
3. Love. So that you can give what God has given you back to Him.

After Gideon dealt with his lack of self-confidence and the voice that had been in his head, he was able to follow the voice of God without hesitation, even when God asked him to do some difficult things. Gideon was on his way to battle with thousands of men, but God told him to send those who were afraid back to their houses. After this, God told him to send more men home based on how they drank water. Gideon was eventually left with three hundred men to go into battle. Look at the verses below to see how Gideon obeyed God.

> *Then Jerubbaal, who is Gideon, and all the people that were with him, rose up early, and pitched beside the well of Harod: so that the host of the Midianites were on the north side of them, by the hill of Moreh, in the valley. And the Lord said unto Gideon, The people that are with thee are too many for me to give the Midianites into their hands, lest Israel vaunt themselves against me, saying, Mine own hand hath saved me. Now therefore go to, proclaim in the ears of the people, saying, Whosoever is fearful and afraid, let him return and depart early from mount Gilead. And there returned of the people twenty and two thousand; and there remained ten thousand. And the Lord said unto Gideon, The people are yet too many; bring them down unto the water, and I will try them for thee there: and it shall be, that of whom I say unto thee, This shall go with thee, the same shall go*

with thee; and of whomsoever I say unto thee, This shall not go with thee, the same shall not go. So he brought down the people unto the water: and the Lord said unto Gideon, Every one that lappeth of the water with his tongue, as a dog lappeth, him shalt thou set by himself; likewise every one that boweth down upon his knees to drink. And the number of them that lapped, putting their hand to their mouth, were three hundred men: but all the rest of the people bowed down upon their knees to drink water. And the Lord said unto Gideon, By the three hundred men that lapped will I save you, and deliver the Midianites into thine hand: and let all the other people go every man unto his place.

~Judges 7:1-7

By breaking free of the voice of uncertainty in himself, Gideon was able to confidently believe God. Gideon was able to become the mighty warrior that God was speaking to when the angel of the Lord had first come to him. The great warrior who was hidden in Gideon eventually came out of him. Gideon now trusted God when the instructions did not make any sense, and he finally grew the confidence that God was ultimately looking for in him. This confidence and obedience led Gideon to the victory for his people. Look at the verse below to see how Gideon delivered the people.

Victory for Gideon

> *Then the men of Israel said unto Gideon, Rule thou over us, both thou, and thy son, and thy son's son also: for thou hast delivered us from the hand of Midian. And Gideon said unto them, I will not rule over you, neither shall my son rule over you: the Lord shall rule over you.*
>
> *~Judges 8:22-23*

After the war with the Midianites, the first thing the children of Israel asked Gideon was for him to rule over them. Gideon confidently declined their offer. He could say this because he wanted to let them know that God would rule over them. This was the testimony of someone who had journeyed with God. He had torn down the altars that had been made to idols, and he'd also worked through the voices that were in his own head, subsequently, defeating the fetal position. Because of this, he developed a trusted relationship with God and partnered with Him to defeat the Midianites. Now, Gideon was returning all the glory back to God, and restoring the people that he had been originally sent to defend. Gideon knew that the last level of love was to not become boastful, but to commit what God wanted back to Him. By committing the people back to God, Gideon completed his assignment.

Here are five points to consider regarding Gideon's journey to overcome insecurity:

1. **God's voice over every other voice** – Prioritize God's voice.
2. **Intercession** – Areas that we may be insecure about are often a burden of intercession of us. For example, if you

are insecure about being bold; boldness is probably a prayer target that should be pushed in prayer. Issues we are insecure about, we can pray about until something happens.

3. **God called him warrior, but he did not see himself as a warrior**- We must remind ourselves daily that we are not called to who we think we are, but who God called us to be. So, we must revisit our encounters with the Lord and the Word of God to allow His Word to speak to our very existence.
4. **Obedience will break anything**- The best way to break free from any mental stronghold is to be obedient. Recall where God may have spoken, and you missed the mark by disobeying Him or you partially obeyed Him. Do what God said for you to do, even if you feel afraid.
5. **Give back to God**- Ultimately, the best sacrifice is giving back to God whatever He gives us. So, if He has called us to be parents, spouses, authors,

entrepreneurs, or whatever titles and responsibilities He has given us, we must find ways to give those gifts back to Him.

Nehemiah was one of those people who was built differently. He spent time praying and believing God for his people. Nehemiah prayed and reminded God that He'd said if His people turned back to Him, He would bring them back into the place He had chosen for them. In his current position, Nehemiah was a cupbearer for the king, but he was also an intercessor for his people. Nehemiah's confidence in God was exhibited in his entire story.

This started with Nehemiah speaking to the king on behalf of his people about rebuilding because this was a burden for him. The king granted Nehemiah his request, but Nehemiah was not satisfied with just the spoken words, so he asked the king to write a letter. Even toward the end of chapter two, Nehemiah had a few people who'd laughed at his plans; they'd tried to scorn him for going against the king.

Nehemiah stood confidently and let them know that all of Heaven was backing him. Nehemiah said with ease, "The God of heaven will prosper us."

Consider the verses below to learn about the background of Nehemiah:

> *O Lord, I beseech thee, let now thine ear be attentive to the prayer of thy servant, and to the prayer of thy servants, who desire to fear thy name: and prosper, I pray thee, thy servant this day, and grant him mercy in the sight of this man. For I was the king's cupbearer.*
>
> *And it came to pass in the month Nisan, in the twentieth year of Artaxerxes the king, that wine was before him: and I took up the wine, and gave it unto the king. Now I had not been beforetime sad in his presence. Wherefore the king said unto me, Why is thy countenance sad, seeing thou art not sick? this is nothing else but sorrow of heart. Then I was very sore afraid, And said unto the king,*

Let the king live for ever: why should not my countenance be sad, when the city, the place of my fathers' sepulchres, lieth waste, and the gates thereof are consumed with fire? Then the king said unto me, For what dost thou make request? So I prayed to the God of heaven. And I said unto the king, If it please the king, and if thy servant have found favour in thy sight, that thou wouldest send me unto Judah, unto the city of my fathers' sepulchres, that I may build it. And the king said unto me, (the queen also sitting by him,) For how long shall thy journey be? And when wilt thou return? So it pleased the king to send me; and I set him a time.
Then answered I them, and said unto them, The God of heaven, he will prosper us; therefore we his servants will arise and build: but ye have no portion, nor right, nor memorial, in Jerusalem.

~Nehemiah 1:11, 2:1-6, 20

When Nehemiah eventually began the work, he had to deal with people who were upset; these people surrounded him and mocked his people. They even conspired against Nehemiah. Nehemiah and his team were on a mission to do the work of the Lord and were unbothered. Many outside voices had something to say about the work that Nehemiah was doing to rebuild Jerusalem, but their words did not send Nehemiah into a fetal position. Instead, these moments created an opportunity for Nehemiah to showcase his faith. Take a look at the passage below:

> *But it came to pass, that when Sanballat heard that we builded the wall, he was wroth, and took great indignation, and mocked the Jews. And he spake before his brethren and the army of Samaria, and said, What do these feeble Jews? will they fortify themselves? will they sacrifice? will they make an end in a day? will they revive the stones out of the heaps of the rubbish which are burned? Now Tobiah the Ammonite was by him, and he said,*

Even that which they build, if a fox go up, he shall even break down their stone wall. Hear, O our God; for we are despised: and turn their reproach upon their own head, and give them for a prey in the land of captivity: And cover not their iniquity, and let not their sin be blotted out from before thee: for they have provoked thee to anger before the builders. So built we the wall; and all the wall was joined together unto the half thereof: for the people had a mind to work.

~Nehemiah 4:1- 6

The commitment and confidence Nehemiah had in God was admirable. Even when the outside voices tried to get him to come down by calling a meeting with him, Nehemiah continued to work and rebuild Jerusalem. He responded to the meeting request by saying, "I am doing a great work. Why should I leave and come down to you?" Wow! During chaos, distraction, and whispers, Nehemiah made up his mind to do the work of the Lord! There was word that there may be an attack, the people continued to rebuild with their swords in one hand and their tools in the other.

When our minds are made up to not be offended, afraid, doubtful, or insecure, there is much God can accomplish through us. Nehemiah's actions were able to easily align with his attitude; this allowed him to continue working despite what was going on around him. Everyone around Nehemiah was equipped with a similar mindset. They recognized that the work of the Lord was too great to allow themselves to be distracted. Consider the verses below:

Confidence

> *Now it came to pass when Sanballat, and Tobiah, and Geshem the Arabian, and the rest of our enemies, heard that I had builded the wall, and that there was no breach left therein; (though at that time I had not set up the doors upon the gates;) That Sanballat and Geshem*

sent unto me, saying, Come, let us meet together in some one of the villages in the plain of Ono. But they thought to do me mischief. And I sent messengers unto them, saying, I am doing a great work, so that I cannot come down: why should the work cease, whilst I leave it, and come down to you?

~Nehemiah 6:1-3

Here are a few points that contributed to Nehemiah's success with the battle of his mind:

1. **Strong prayer life**- Nehemiah consistently prayed and sought out the mind of God. This ultimately gave him another level of discernment to understand the difference between the voice of God and the voice of an imposter.
2. **Commitment to the burden** – The Lord gave Nehemiah a burden, and he remained committed to that burden until the project was completed in its entirety. Nehemiah was not anxious, nor did he

worry. He was confident that God would prosper them.

3. **Don't forget God's promise**- Nehemiah reminded God of His promise to His people. Nehemiah did what God loves; he held Him accountable to His Word.
4. **Speak in Faith** – Everything about Nehemiah was in alignment, including his actions and his words. What Nehemiah was speaking is also what he was praying, believing, and doing.
5. **Believe God** – Nehemiah was committed to believing God at His Word. What had God promised him? That He would back them regardless of if they had the king's approval. He was in complete trust of God in the presence of his enemies.
6. **Have the mind to work**- Although Nehemiah was technically waiting on God for deliverance, he got to work and partnered with God. He and his men were committed to the project.

7. **Do not stop until it happens** – The team kept going until the project was complete. They literally saw the impossible become possible through faith. What started out as a simple prayer from Nehemiah ended up being a significant moment in history when the walls were rebuilt for the city of Jerusalem.

Gideon Versus Nehemiah

So, we looked at two completely different leaders and their journeys. Gideon started out insecure and afraid, but over time, he was able to work through the voices in his head and build trust in God. Nehemiah began with intercession, faith, and hope. He was totally convinced that God would do what He said He would do. For Nehemiah, there was no need to deal with any internal voices; instead, he had to utilize his confidence to overcome the outside influences and distractions. Gideon ended up in the fetal position after he'd received a message from the angel of the Lord. Nehemiah reminded and approached God about the word that had been spoken regarding His people. He reminded Him of what He'd said He was going to do. Gideon was eventually able to obey God's word for word in each instruction the Lord gave him regarding the battle. Nehemiah stepped out on a word and never looked back.

We can allow the fetal position, voices, emotions, grief, and hardships to rob us of our rightful places in God, or we can put those emotions/ situations in their perspective places and be confident in the work that the Lord has already begun in us (Philippians 1:6). Being confident of this very thing, that he which hath begun a good work in you will perform it until the day of Jesus Christ.

Whether we are feeling like Gideon or Nehemiah, please remember that both were able to be used by God to ultimately accomplish His work. Just find a way to defeat every other voice that tries to hinder you, and allow God's voice to be the dominant voice in your life.

Chapter 6

(Loneliness)

In our lifetimes, most of us have experienced loneliness at some point. This is either because we were not able to be around people or we were around others but felt alone. There are many definitions of the word loneliness. Let us look at a few from a few different sources:

1. Loneliness is an unpleasant emotional response to perceived isolation. Loneliness is also described as social pain—a psychological mechanism which motivates individuals to seek social connections. (Wikipedia)
2. Loneliness is the state of distress or discomfort that results when one perceives a gap between one's desires for social connection and

actual experiences of it. (Psychology Today)

3. In "A Biography of Loneliness: The History of an Emotion" (Oxford), the British historian Fay Bound Alberti defines loneliness as "a conscious, cognitive feeling of estrangement or social separation from meaningful others," and she objects to the idea that it's universal, transhistorical, and the source of all that ails us. Loneliness is grief distended. Loneliness is a state of profound distress. Loneliness is the feeling that no place is home. (Wall Street Journal)

From these three sources, we have gathered that loneliness is an internal and emotional response that often keeps us from having meaningful relationships. Loneliness can be extended based on our perspectives. We can begin to see ourselves or our situations from the lens of loneliness if we commit to the pain long enough. There are many reasons someone may feel lonely. We can deal with loneliness and not realize that loneliness is affecting us.

Three out of five Americans reported that they are lonely, according to NPR. They reported that they felt left out, poorly understood or they had a lack of companionship. A big contributor to loneliness is the culture at a person's place of work. People need a sense of belonging at work, otherwise, they will experience loneliness in the workplace. Many times, the most challenging piece of being lonely is that we feel isolated and that no one else is dealing with a similar emotion.

NPR also surveyed ten thousand people and found that the feelings of being alone were present in all generations, including Generation Z, not just older folks. Also, more men felt alone than women, which was surprising. Those who used social media more heavily seemed to have greater issues with loneliness, as opposed to light social media users. Lastly, those who had good co-worker relationships reported being less lonely than those who had a great work-life balance.

The state of feeling alone can be connected to anxiety and depression. Most times, the battle is just in our minds. Feeling alone can be contributed to overthinking, being over-analytical, and allowing false narratives to play in our minds. Sometimes, we may make the effort to communicate where we are to others, but feel like those around us are not hearing us or that they misunderstand our communication. After many failed attempts to communicate, the easiest thing to do is just shut down, however, this is healthy soil for loneliness to grow.

The life of Joseph gives us a great perspective of how loneliness can enter our lives. All the same, he is an example of how to overcome loneliness. Consider the verses below:

And when they saw him afar off, even before he came near unto them, they conspired against him to slay him. And they said one to another, Behold, this dreamer cometh. Come now therefore, and let us slay him, and cast him into some pit, and we will say, Some evil beast hath devoured him: and we shall see what will become of his dreams. And Reuben heard it, and he delivered him out of their hands; and said, Let us not kill him. And Reuben said unto them, Shed no blood, but cast him into this pit that is in the wilderness, and lay no hand upon him; that he might rid him out of their hands, to deliver him to his father again. And it came to pass, when Joseph was come unto his brethren, that they stript Joseph out of his coat, his coat of many colours that was on him; And they took him, and cast him into a pit: and the pit was empty, there was no water in it. And they sat down to eat bread: and they lifted up their eyes and looked, and, behold, a company of Ishmeelites came from Gilead with their camels bearing spicery and balm and myrrh, going to carry it down to Egypt. And Judah said unto his brethren, What profit is it if we slay our brother, and conceal his blood? Come, and let us sell him to the Ishmeelites, and let not our hand be upon him; for he is our brother and our flesh. And his brethren were content. Then there passed by Midianites merchantmen; and they drew and lifted up Joseph out of the pit, and sold Joseph to the Ishmeelites for twenty pieces of silver: and they brought Joseph into Egypt. And Reuben returned unto the pit; and, behold, Joseph was not in the pit; and he rent his clothes. And he returned unto his brethren, and said, The child is not; and I, whither shall I go? And they took Joseph's coat, and killed a kid of the goats, and dipped the coat in the blood; And they sent the coat of many colours, and they brought it to their father; and said, This have we found: know now whether it be thy son's coat or no. And he knew it, and said, It is my son's coat; an evil beast hath devoured him; Joseph is without doubt rent in pieces. And Jacob rent his clothes, and put sackcloth upon his loins, and mourned for his son many days. And all his sons and all his daughters rose up to comfort him; but he refused to be comforted; and he said, For I will go down into the grave unto my son mourning. Thus his father wept for him. And the Midianites sold him into Egypt unto Potiphar, an officer of Pharaoh's, and captain of the guard.

~Genesis 37:18:36

Joseph was born as the eleventh child in a family of twelve children. His father had multiple wives, but the one his father adored was Rachel, Joseph's mother. Joseph was his father's favorite child, and his dad made that known. His brothers were very envious of their relationship; it was extremely difficult for them to process. Joseph found himself having a few dreams where the Lord shared with him about his future. Joseph shared those dreams with his family. His brothers were completely jealous of him and his position within his family so much so that they devised a plan to get rid of him. Joseph's brothers hated him so much that they did not want him to live.

One of his brothers spoke up and convinced the other brothers to sell him into slavery, instead of killing him. Joseph ended up being taken from his family, thrown into a pit, and then sold off into slavery. In a matter of moments, Joseph was snatched from his community, his family, and most importantly, the love of his father. Some of us can relate to this level of separation, but others can only imagine how this could feel.

Joseph had dreams that looked nothing like his reality. He had a few stops to make along the way to his purpose, including the pit and the prison. He would find himself in these low places until he finally reached his promise.

What may have caused Joseph to deal with loneliness? There are three sources mentioned below:

1. **Separation from family** – Joseph was suddenly pulled from his family, and he had no idea if he would ever see them again. The place where he grew up, his parents, his siblings were all gone. He then found himself in an unknown land and in an uncertain place.
2. **His brothers played a role in his separation** -This could have easily allowed the feelings of rejection to surface which, of course, leads us down another path to loneliness. If his own family could treat him this way, what would others do? How could he trust anyone to care for him? How many of us deal with this type of loneliness? This form of loneliness derives from family drama or trauma that has caused us to isolate ourselves and retreat from any type of meaningful relationship.
3. **How would Joseph survive all of this?** How could he have hope after all

> of this? God had shown him some amazing dreams, but he ended up in a place of hopelessness. Joseph may have thought that he was far from what God had revealed to him, but he was closer than he had ever been. Losing hope is an event that we all have faced, and hopelessness has the power to drive us into loneliness. Some of us have lost hope in our dreams because of where we are. Consequently, we now feel lonely. The uncertainty of tomorrow and the unknown of today causes anxiety, and this anxiety allows for the feelings of loneliness to surface.

Can you see yourself as Joseph in an unknown land and culture, trying to figure everything out? Have you ever had a moment in your family where you felt ostracized? For whatever reason, everyone else thought or did something different than you were doing! Maybe you were still physically around your family or even your friends, but you felt far from them. The feeling of being alone can easily become our reality when separation hits, whether that be in the physical or in our minds.

Joseph handled his journey with loneliness well. He gave us keys to overcoming the feeling of being alone. He basically taught us how to overcome loneliness within ourselves. Check out the three points below:

1. **Good moral**- Joseph did not allow his circumstances to dictate his attitude or his approach. He held on to his integrity and was honest. This allowed him to be prosperous wherever he landed. Joseph maintained a positive outlook on life and worked hard. He was not overtaken by the thoughts of being alone.
2. **Kept working**- Joseph did the work that was in front of him and let God handle the rest. While there were many questions to be concerned with, he kept his work ethic and did what was required of him. Would he ever see his parents again? How would he mange his relationship with his brothers? Many thoughts could have been swimming

through his mind, but he found meaning in his work and pressed on.

3. **Forgiveness** – The biggest key to overcoming loneliness is often forgiveness. We are often pushed into loneliness by offense or the feelings of being misunderstood. So, forgiveness will easily unlock the door of loneliness and allow you to have healthier relationships. Now, that does not mean we always have to allow the offenders back into our spaces, but we do need to let them out of the mental prisons we've placed them in.

Let us look at the passage below to see how Joseph handled finally seeing his family again:

> *Then Joseph could not refrain himself before all them that stood by him; and he cried, Cause every man to go out from me. And there stood no man with him, while Joseph made himself known unto his brethren. And he wept aloud: and the Egyptians and the house of*

> *Pharaoh heard. And Joseph said unto his brethren, I am Joseph; doth my father yet live? And his brethren could not answer him; for they were troubled at his presence. And Joseph said unto his brethren, Come near to me, I pray you. And they came near. And he said, I am Joseph your brother, whom ye sold into Egypt. Now therefore be not grieved, nor angry with yourselves, that ye sold me hither: for God did send me before you to preserve life.*
>
> *~Genesis 45:1-5*

Hence why I love Joseph's story! As soon as he saw his brothers, he cried because he loved and missed them. He had a heart of forgiveness towards the same people who'd caused him to be in the fetal position. The interesting part is that his brothers were now in a fetal position because of the famine in the land, and the person in charge of the resources was their brother. Joseph quickly disarmed them by letting them know that it was all God's plan so that they would not suffer. He told them not to be grieved because what the enemy intended for evil, God turned the situation around for their good.

What an exciting testimony to look forward to in our own lives! The very thing that was meant to break us down and send us into the fetal position was there to bring us into a place of prosperity and a great expected end. Joseph represents all of us. At some point in our lives, we will feel isolated and alone, but Joseph gave us hope, reminding us that if we stay the course, God will turn our tests into beautiful testimonies.

When I was twenty-five years old, I had just finished my first Master's degree. I decide to take a job offer in Indianapolis, Indiana. I had never heard of this city, plus I was from a big city. Most of my family lived on the east coast. I recall announcing that I was moving to Indiana. Funny enough, one of my relatives thought I was moving to India. I had to explain many times that Indiana was a part of the Midwest, near Illinois and Ohio.

I remember the exact day I decided to board the plane to Indianapolis. I shipped my car to the city, and the movers packed and shipped my things. I boarded the plane with two suitcases and a dream. I landed in Indianapolis and retrieved my suitcases from the baggage claim terminal. Suddenly, a wave of loneliness hit me. I was separated from my family, I had nowhere to go, and no way to get there. I needed to pick my car up from the house of someone who, at the time, was almost a stranger to me. To make matters worse, my apartment was not going to be available for another two weeks. I had only traveled maybe three times by myself, one of which was to interview for a job.

I just sat in the airport right next to baggage claim terminal and cried. What had I done? I had just left my family, my city, and my place of familiarity, and I'd launched out into the deep. How would I recover? Would I meet anyone? Would I connect with people? Where would I eat? Would I eat alone every night? Would people even come to visit me here? So many thoughts flooded my mind. Finally, I found my peace, put together a plan for my next steps and moved forward. Yes, I felt lonely for a moment, but I soon realized I had to get up from there. I made the choice to follow the direction I felt that God was leading me in my life.

Eventually, I was able to connect with many people in Indiana who became like family to me. Everything I needed and more was provided to me in my time there. I just had to get past the initial feelings of being alone. On the other side of that loneliness was so much more.

In this transition to Indiana, I was able to put the principles that Joseph outlined for us in his journey of overcoming loneliness:

1. **Good Moral**- I maintained integrity in my time in Indiana by being accountable to my church and family. Also, I kept a positive mindset, knowing that all things were working together for my good.

2. **Kept Working** – I found meaningful work at church and in my day job. I was able to also serve as a volunteer in under-served communities.
3. **Forgiveness** – I found space and time to forgive those who'd offended me throughout this transition. Lastly, I had to forgive myself for the things and people I left behind to be open to the new things God was doing in my life.

Oftentimes, we worry ourselves and delay our own transitions because of the frustrations, offenses, fears, and everything that surfaces whenever one season comes to an end. Transitions can bring on loneliness, fear, doubt, and many other emotions. Let this scripture encourage our spirits, knowing that better is the end of a thing than the beginning of a thing. Knowing that whatever work that Jesus started in us, He will finish. We must also renew our perspectives concerning transitions to allow ourselves to see that there is purpose in the ending.

Better is the end of a thing than the beginning thereof: and the patient in spirit is better than the proud in spirit.

~Ecclesiastes 7:8

Chapter 7

(The Transition)

The great examples of Abraham gave us so much insight when we discussed doubt in chapter four. One major point we missed was where the doubt originated. How could a man of great faith have any place for doubt in his life? Abraham, who at the time of his upbringing, was named Abram had been born into a people group called the Chaldeans. The Chaldeans were known for idol worship. Idol worship, at that time, was when there was a tangible object being created for people to worship as their god or gods. These idols would have some symbolic representations of what people imagined their god or gods to be.

Scripture tells us about doubting. Consider the story of Thomas, where Jesus said to Thomas, "You have seen me and believed, but blessed are those that have not seen me and believed." This brings about a principle; people who tend to worship idols have some form of doubt lingering in their minds. This is evidenced in the fact that they need a god that they can see, hence the need for a physical being to represent God in the Earth. Take a look at the passage below:

> *Then saith he to Thomas, Reach hither thy finger, and behold my hands; and reach hither thy hand, and thrust it into my side: and be not faithless, but believing. And Thomas answered and said unto him, My Lord and my God. Jesus saith unto him, Thomas, because thou hast seen me, thou hast believed: blessed are they that have not seen, and yet have believed.*
>
> *~John 20:27-29*

So, here we have Abraham, a man who has made great strides in his faith journey amid a situation where doubt creeps into his mind. Why was doubt able to creep in? There was an open door left in his mind from his family. Even though he had left the environment of idol worshipers, there was still some residue of his past present. He had an inherent intuition to doubt God at His Word. Abraham had an extensive history with God. God had kept him and allowed him to make major moves in the Earth, but Abraham was concerned about the promise of a son.

We can so easily get so caught up with the promise that we forget the character of the One who made the promise. Remember, He is not a God that He would lie. Whatever God said, He will do. He does not need us trying to make the promises happen for ourselves. Abram was distracted for a moment and felt the need to help God honor His own Word by having a son with Sarai's maid.

There is an even bigger idea to focus on in the journey of Abraham; that is the constant transitioning he had to deal with in his journey with the Lord. His first step was to follow a set of almost empty instructions; the Lord had told him to leave his place of familiarity and to go into an unknown land. Even after leaving his country, the instructions were not clear as to what he was to do next or where he was going, but he was to follow the Lord. The Lord literally said, “Go into a land that I will show you.” So, without seeing, Abram had to make a move to follow the Lord.

> *Now the Lord had said unto Abram, Get thee out of thy country, and from thy kindred, and from thy father's house, unto a land that I will shew thee:*
>
> *~Genesis 12:1*

Abraham’s life can serve as a model for transition. Transitioning has many challenges and emotions that come along with it. We never really hear much about the difficulties of transitioning; we just glorify the blessing or mourn the loss, but never deal with the significant changes that may have happened in our lives during our transitions.

Transition is the process or a period of changing from one state or condition to another (Oxford Languages Dictionary). The process of transitioning can be either good, bad, or downright ugly. Some people may be experiencing seasons of new things, like getting a new job, house, or car, or they may be entering new relationships, friendships, or even growing their families. Then again, others may be experiencing not-so-pleasant transitions such as loss, grief, repossession, divorce, or illness. We all must deal with some degree of transitioning in our lives; some may be more challenging than others.

Let us take a closer look at Abraham's journey with transitioning and how his life was impacted. So, at the time, his name was Abram. He decided to move on the Word of the Lord at seventy-five years old; this was after he'd already lived a full life, and he was now at an age where most people retire. Abram decided to follow the Word of the Lord while in a season when many things in life were familiar to him, plus he was surrounded by friends and family members. He left all that he knew and went to a place that was completely unfamiliar to him. Take a look at the passage below:

Now the Lord had said unto Abram, Get thee out of thy country, and from thy kindred, and from thy father's house, unto a land that I will shew thee: And I will make of thee a great nation, and I will bless thee, and make thy name great; and thou shalt be a blessing: And I will bless them that bless thee, and curse him that curseth thee: and in thee shall all families of the earth be blessed. So Abram departed, as the Lord had spoken unto him; and Lot went with him: and Abram was seventy and five years old when he departed out of Haran. And Abram took Sarai his wife, and Lot his brother's son, and all their substance that they had gathered, and the souls that they had gotten in Haran; and they went forth to go into the land of Canaan; and into the land of Canaan they came.

~Genesis 12:1-5

God told Abram to leave, promising that He would make him great nation, bless him, make his name great, and allow him to be a blessing. The Lord also informed him that He would curse those that cursed him and bless those that blessed him. Abram was facing the ultimate decision—should he transition based on the Word of the Lord or stay with what he had always known? Of course, Abram decided to leave and to journey with the Lord, tossing himself in a constant state of transitioning.

Now Abram's transitions were physical; he moved from one place to several others, but what does transition look like in our own lives? Some of us are affected deeply by the thought of transitioning. First, let us look at a few transitions that we may find ourselves in:

1. **Relocation** – we choose to move, or we are forced to move because of the circumstances we find ourselves facing. We are compelled, forced and instructed to move to another country, state, city, or neighborhood.
2. **Death** – someone close to us dies.

3. **New house, car, job, school, church** – we decide to get something new in one or all these areas.
4. **Relationships** – we are constantly either losing friends or gaining new friends.
5. **Mindsets/ appetites/ diets** – leaving old mindsets and recalibrating your desires that would allow you to fit into a plan, a dress, a suit, a relationship, or a new reality.
6. **Losing house, car, job, school, or church** – because of repossession or just facing difficulties in life, we lose some of the very things that oftentimes define us.
7. **Faith** – some may decide they no longer want to go to church, or they may decide to embrace a new religion. Then again, some people may decide to leave religion as a whole to satisfy some deep longing in their souls.

Many of us have faced these types of transitions in one way or another. We have dealt with the grief of losing a loved one, but may not have faced the changes in our lives due to death. When a person leaves us, our lives are forever changed, and we move internally to a different state. There is an interaction we can no longer have, and we are left with the memories we shared with that loved one. These types of transitions leave a vacancy in our lives. When we get a new job or house, we move forward internally and have a newfound responsibility. We think differently, and this transition can honestly sometimes be overwhelming. Consequently, when transitioning is a choice, most are hesitant or reluctant to go forward with the transition.

Let's talk more about those willful transitions versus forced transitions. Most people are accustomed to forced transitions as opposed to willful ones. People transitioning based on a choice are rare. Usually, the circumstances we find ourselves in bring about most forced transitions. One of the things I am personally used to is changing or moving based on a decision. You will be surprised how many people wait until things are unbearably bad before they will leave a relationship or job.

Earlier in this chapter, I mentioned the job I'd moved to Indiana, and get this, I eventually left that job. There was nothing wrong; everything was going well. I was making good money and had great relationships and mentors, but like Abram, I had a word. There was something I felt God had spoken to me concerning my future. I felt that the transition was needed for me to journey with the Lord. You see, I like Abram's story of transition because I feel like him all the time. So, I put in a six months' notice and left a job that most people would have been happy to make a career out of. This was a choice I felt I needed to make to really fulfill my life's call.

In the book *Culture of Honor*, Danny Silk shares a principle and a practice with us based on Abraham's story. It is a wealth mindset principle called "leaving your father's house." He wants us to realize that we have been impacted and affected by what was seen as normal to us and our families. These are the people who set the standards in our lives. While these factors do not control us, they do affect us. Here, we see that there is significance in transitioning, whether it be physical or spiritual, because whenever we transition, there is a change to our mindsets.

Understanding the principle of leaving our father's houses helps us to learn God's assignment for us based on the environments He places us in. Danny Silk mentioned that in Genesis 12:1, God showed Abram that He wanted to change his mind by changing his surroundings. Silk goes on to share these three things that God had him leave:

1. **Country. This represented his physical limitations.**
2. **Family. This represented the limitations surrounding his self-concept.**
3. **Father's house. This represented his socioeconomic limitations.**

Abram left each of these things behind him. He left the place where he'd grown up and he left his family behind. With these, he left the familiarity of everything that shaped how he saw himself based on his family's standards. This is like when we only see ourselves as the nicknames our families gave us, and not the way that God sees us. Ultimately, after dealing with the residue of doubt, he left his father's house or the economic path that was set before him. He traded it all in for a real intimate worship encounter with God. In exchange for Abram's decision to allow God to transform his mind, God blessed him, made him the father of many nations, and allowed his name to be great on the Earth.

While changing from one state to another can be initiated by many events (especially when we are submitted to the direction and plans God has for us), there is something on the other side of the change that God wants to use to develop our character. This would enable us to handle the weight of what God is trying to accomplish through us. The change is just the training or the beginning of what God is trying to do in us. Transitioning will allow us to access wisdom that we never thought was available to us because we initially didn't have that degree of access and opportunity.

Another major transition in the Bible is in the year King Uzziah died. King Uzziah was a great king in the Bible. He started his reign at age sixteen. He was known for his faithfulness towards God, and because of his faithfulness, he was rewarded with great strength. Howbeit, because of his strength, he was known to become proud. Eventually, King Uzziah tried to burn incense in the temple; this was an act that was reserved for priests only. When he did this, he was immediately struck with leprosy and became very ill.

During the reign of King Uzziah, there was a prophet named Isaiah. Isaiah had visions and would receive words from the Lord, but he was not really known to most as a prophet; that was until Isaiah 6:1:

In the year that king Uzziah died I saw also the Lord sitting upon a throne, high and lifted up, and his train filled the temple.

King Uzziah's passing was a very disappointing time for the people he'd ruled over. King Uzziah was a great and wise king who'd made a mistake. During these times, great leadership was few and far between, so the people really valued the leadership of King Uzziah. This was a difficult transition for the people and for Isaiah. Currently, Isaiah was at the place of discovery regarding the call that was on his life. This was the type of news that likely put Isaiah in the fetal position.

In Isaiah 6:1, Isaiah experienced a supernatural encounter with God. He saw the Lord high and lifted. He exalted the Lord in his moment of transitioning and pain. Isaiah traded in his sorrows for the joy of the Lord and was able to receive the seal of the Lord on his ministry. What greater way to commission Isaiah than for God Himself to show up and His glory to fill the temple! The Lord also spoke to him during that time and told him to go and speak to the people; this way, they would be completely healed. Isaiah should have been discouraged at this moment, after all, the king had died, but God sent him to encourage the people.

I declare for those of you that are reading this and may be in a season of transition, pain, or grief that God will be exalted in this moment of your life. I declare that in this time of changing from one place to the next, you will encounter God, and that this time, your pain will be used for God's glory. In this time of transition, you will encounter God like you never have before if you seek Him. I believe that even in reading this book, you will receive an Isaiah type of encounter that in a place and time where you should be discouraged, God will send you out to encourage others. You are making yourself available and ready to glorify the Father.

While a period of change can be difficult, we can see through Abraham's decision and Isaiah's grief that there is a blessing on the other side of transition. Though the moment may be painful, and weeping may endure for a night, joy will come in the morning. Be encouraged and reminded that if you will lift God up in your seasons of transition, He will draw near to you. The Bible says in Isaiah 55:6, "Seek the Lord while he may be found and call on him while he is near." In our lowest times, God is close, and I promise you He is not afraid of your suffering or sadness. He is the Son of suffering. He wore our issues so that we could experience freedom here on Earth.

Just remember that in transition, there are five points that will unfold:

1. **Changed mindset** – New wine can't go into old wineskins, so for us to receive the new mindset that God desires for us, we must shed our sense of normalcy and be prepared to change our mindset.

2. **Access granted-** Isaiah was able to connect with God in ways he had never done before after the king died. For some of us, the transition does not have to be death, but simply leaving out of our fathers' houses will create a point of access that we've never had before. I remember when I moved to Indiana, I started to have a relationship with God I had never been able to access in times past. This is because I was once comfortable with leaning on the relationship my parents had with God; that was enough for me. But after being in Indiana alone with God, I realized that there was nothing like knowing Him for myself.
3. **Makes room** – Proverbs says your gift will make room for you and bring you into the presence of great men. There is a transition happening here in this verse. The gift has matured and become disciplined, therefore, there is a demand for space to be created. Transitions also occur when we matriculate or move

from one level to the next, and that maturation creates space.

4. **Brings on freedom** – Who the Son sets free is free indeed. There is a transactional transition that happens as well. When you receive the love of the Father, you break out of your bondage to sin and shame and you move towards freedom!
5. **Discovery**-There is time in the discovery phase where we are isolated. This is when we must take time to discover God and discover ourselves. Discovery is like becoming a kid again and seeing the world from a different perspective. Children are often excited by the simple things. Sometimes, in transition, our minds are easily clouded by the challenges we are dealing with, but through the lens of discovery, we learn to see the new details. We may find joy, peace, or something to be thankful for through discovery. I became a runner in Indiana, even though most people think I ran in college

and high school. I started running at twenty-five during my transitional phase. It was then that I discovered that I love running. Running has helped to better my mental health; it is a hobby that gives me time to process and think things through more deeply. Additionally, running allows me to get past myself and to see beyond my thoughts. God is with us in transition; remember to seek Him in these moments.

Seek ye the LORD while he may be found, call ye upon him while he is near.
~Isaiah 55:6

Chapter 8

(It is Already Done!)

Bless the LORD, O my soul, and forget not all his benefits: Who forgiveth all thine iniquities; who healeth all thy diseases; Who redeemeth thy life from destruction; who crowneth thee with lovingkindness and tender mercies; Who satisfieth thy mouth with good things; so that thy youth is renewed like the eagle's.

~Psalms 103:2- 5

Being a child of God, there are certain benefits that we have access to since He is our Father. If we were employed at a certain job, we would ask what are in the benefits package. The employer would then list off several things, like vacation days, maternity or paternity leave, gym membership, stocks, and many other benefits that they give employees. Having accepted Jesus as our Lord and Savior, there are special benefits that we are able to utilize in this journey of life. Let's review the outline of some of the benefits that we have access to through the finished work of Jesus Christ.

1. **He forgives our sins.**
2. **He heals us from diseases.**
3. **He redeems us from hell.**
4. **He crowns us with love and mercy.**
5. **He wraps us in goodness.**
6. **He renews our youth.**

The benefits listed above are a part of being in a relationship with Jesus. When we come into relationship with Jesus, we learn about the love He has for the world. This love is so potent that He gave His life so that we could be free. Through Him going to the cross for us, there was work completed that allowed us to live life differently.

When we say the finished work of Jesus, the Christ, we are talking about what Jesus did on to the cross. Sometimes, what happened on the cross is overlooked or underestimated. We see the cross as something Jesus did, but we do not understand how that impacts our lives right now. Being able to make the connection is essential to the foundation of our faith. The understanding of the cross fundamentally gives us a transformative perspective on how we can live better lives each day.

I grew up in a very traditional church. When I say traditional, I mean that there were many rules surrounding what women could not do, like wear makeup, pants, etc. For me, being a child growing up in this environment, the way I processed the rules was I believed that I was saved based on my ability to comply with the rules. Every day, I would measure myself and others based on the set of rules that had been given to us. I did not really make a connection between what Jesus did on the cross with my life and the rules. The rules became my main focus in developing a relationship with the Lord.

Later in life, I developed my own personal relationship with the Lord. During that time, I realized that rules that I needed to adhere to in my relationship with God were more so based on the roles and responsibilities God was calling me to adhere to. I started to understand how Jesus going to the cross forever impacted my life and how my beliefs would shift my future.

Growing up, there was always a natural tension between my upbringing and what I dreamed of becoming in the future. I am an administrative person, naturally gifted in leadership who, at times, can be very vocal. This is because I grew up in a space where women were to be quiet in the church and never really have any real place in leadership within the church. So, I could never see where I would fit in with my dreams. This tension existed until I found my relationship with God. When I found my relationship with God, I began a journey with the Holy Spirit. In this journey, I was able to reconcile my faith and my heart back to my dreams. I was able to put away thoughts of worry, anxiety, doubt, and fear. I stopped looking for acceptance from people and started walking in my acceptance with God. I decided to accept the fact that I am justified by my faith and not my works.

I no longer measured myself by the rules that were taught to me. I learned to mature in my relationship with the Lord by spending time with Him. As I matured, I understood more of my role, rights, and responsibilities in the relationship. With that understanding, I was freed from the pressures associated with missing the mark and the fear of not meeting the expectations of man.

Maybe, you have a certain dream for your life, but you have no exposure in that area. Like me, you may be in the very environment that opposes your dreams. For example, you desire to be a singer, but no one in your family is a singer. Another example is, you desire to be a basketball player, but for whatever reason, this is despised by your family. You find yourself like me, asking God, "Why would you put me in an environment that was not fit for your call?" The environment we are raised in may not seem as if it fits our call based on the tangibles, but there is something being deposited in us to ultimately get us to where God wants us.

Think back to when we discussed Joseph in the earlier chapters. God was giving him these great dreams about his purpose and calling in life. However, none of his brothers could see his dreams coming true. Instead, they became jealous and decided that they were better off without Joseph in their lives. Joseph ended up in a pit, then he became a slave, and he eventually ended up in jail. This took place before he was able to see clearly why each of these processes was important. This happened to him even before he was able to reconcile why he had been born into that particular family. There was a natural tension between who Joseph was called to be and his upbringing, but he ultimately realized that he had been born into his family for a reason. That reason, of course, was to save them from the famine. He also determined that every low moment in his life was necessary to bring about the character for the assignment God had for him.

For some of us, God is getting ready to reconcile our pasts and futures. You may have thought that there was a significant delay in your process and that this delay was keeping you from your future. But you are getting ready to see the delay was needed and that God is the Author of time. Even time bows to Him; ask Joshua. Joshua prayed and asked God to hold the sun for him so they could continue to fight. I pray that everything that has kept you from getting to where God is calling you to be catapults you into your purpose, both exceedingly and abundantly, above all you can ask or think.

There was a tension between who I was and who I felt God was calling me to become during my upbringing. It wasn't until I'd left my place of familiarity and comfort that I discovered the grace on my life to do exactly what I believe God was sharing with me concerning my life. I had to first come into agreement with the work of Christ and understanding that by faith we receive salvation.

First, I had to challenge my belief system or how I had been programmed in my upbringing. Next, I had to challenge what I believed about myself, so that regardless of the circumstance I found myself in, there would always be an internal force keeping me on the journey. That force was my faith in God and my faith in myself. By partnering with the Holy Spirit, I came to the realization that I could never please God by my works, but by faith. I was already pleasing to God in who I am, but my faith is what made an impression on my ability to trust Him. Just imagine a father being excited by his young daughter's ability to trust him. So, the little girl just jumps into her father's arms without restraint, fear, or hesitancy. In the most freeing way, the child is confident that no matter what, the love of the father will catch her and keep her safe.

The following two verses really speak to the love of God and how our faith connects us to Him.

> *Therefore being justified by faith, we have peace with God through our Lord Jesus Christ:*
>
> *~Romans 5:1*

> *But God demonstrates his own love for us in this: While we were still sinners, Christ died for us.*
>
> *~Romans 5:8*

By faith, we are justified; this allows us to be in right-standing with Christ, and it allows us to be fit for Him and the works that He has for us. While I was looking for my environment to be the right fit, He was bringing me into and fitting me for the right place. This way, I would be at peace with who I am because of Him and what He has done for me. While I was trying to discover God, I learned that God had been intentionally drawing me. My timing began to align with His timing, and I discovered that He already knew me. Eventually, I understood my placement with Him. I came to understand that I was accepted by Him. I was what He wanted all along. Ultimately, my decision would allow the Father to be glorified through my life.

While we were in sin, God demonstrated the amazing act of love for us. He died so that we could live and have life more abundantly. This is so that we could live free of the emotions that try to hold us in bondage or keep us out of our destinies. My dad shared something with me that has always resonated with me. Imagine a woman in the hospital giving birth to a child, and the father of her child is out somewhere cheating on her. While he is committing this act, she is giving life in one of the most painful and powerful ways. The man is obviously not thinking of her, but she has put everything into this moment of birthing a child into this world.

God had us on His mind when we had no consideration of Him or His heart towards us. His plan, all along, was to bring us back into right-standing with Him. He did not want us to go through certain things, so He created a way for us to be victorious. The love of the Father has so many dimensions. God had a plan to reconcile humanity after the fall. Most of us know that there were blood sacrifices that had to be made after Adam fell into sin. There was a list of the type of blood sacrifices that needed to be made to omit the sins.

For the sins to be forgiven for all of humanity, God sent Himself in human form as His Son, Jesus, the Christ. These two verses speak to God's love for us, and what He did through Jesus so that we could be made righteous with Him.

> *For God so loved the world, that he gave his only begotten Son, that whosoever believeth in him should not perish, but have everlasting life.*
>
> *~John 3:16*

> *For he hath made him to be sin for us, who knew no sin; that we might be*

made the righteousness of God in him.
~2 Corinthians 5:21

Jesus had no sins. He was perfect; however, He took on our imperfections at the cross. He could have gotten off the cross and did something else. Even when it was painful, overwhelming, and inconvenient, the price was still worth it. He did this so that we could have everlasting life, without being disconnected from the Father because of sin.

Check out the verses below about His desire for us to have a new life in Him:

For the love of Christ constraineth us; because we thus judge, that if one died for all, then were all dead: And that he died for all, that they which live should not henceforth live unto themselves, but unto him which died for them, and rose again. Wherefore henceforth know we no man after the flesh: yea, though we have known Christ after the flesh, yet now henceforth know we him no more. Therefore if any man be in Christ, he is a new creature: old things are passed away; behold, all things are become new. And all things are of God, who hath reconciled us to himself by Jesus Christ, and hath given to us the ministry of reconciliation; To wit, that God was in Christ, reconciling the world unto himself, not imputing their trespasses unto them; and hath committed unto us the word of reconciliation. Now then we are ambassadors for Christ, as though God did beseech you by us: we pray you in Christ's stead, be ye reconciled to God. For he hath made him to be sin for us, who knew no sin; that we might be made the righteousness of God in him.

~2 Corinthians 5:14-21

So, God not only had a desire for us to receive reconciliation, but for us to be ministers of reconciliation. Instead of us being judged by what we have or what we look like, God looks at our hearts. Since we were included in His decision to go to the cross, we are included in the new life after the cross. A new life that is much better than what we would have had without Jesus, and we will enjoy a fresh start because of our allegiance with Jesus.

This forever impacts our ability to be locked in a room in a fetal position. In times where most people would be overwhelmed with emotions and sadness, we will have joy because, regardless of how we feel, we know that there is a posture that we've received in our spirits through Christ. This posture is our positional place of peace, joy, and praise because there is never a need for someone else to come in these moments of difficulty with us, since the love of the Father has already gone there with us and before us. He dealt with sin, death, and hell all at the same time. Sin being the things that would try to take us out of position with Christ, death being the things that would try to kill us, and hell being the things that would try to torment us. As my pastor, Apostle Bryan Meadows, notes, there is significance in the number three. Here is a chart he created below.

Thirty-Fold	Sixty -Fold	One Hundred Fold
Holy Spirit	Sin	Father
Sin	Death	Hell
Steal	Kill	Destroy

We could go on about the significance of the number three in the scriptures. The number three represents the completeness of a thing. It also represents prophetic fulfillment, which denotes how God will complete the process in us.

One of the most significant moments at the cross is when Jesus uttered the words, "It is finished." Many times, we have heard messages like these spoken at the Good Friday services, but I just want to submit this phrase to you one more time. Let us look at this passage from one of the disciples:

> *After this, Jesus knowing that all things were now accomplished, that the scripture might be fulfilled, saith, I thirst.*

> *Now there was set a vessel full of vinegar: and they filled a spunge with vinegar, and put it upon hyssop, and put it to his mouth. When Jesus therefore had received the vinegar, he said,* ***It is finished****: and he bowed his head, and gave up the ghost.*
>
> *~John 19: 28-30*

Even though we may be experiencing the pain of transition, along with fear, doubt, insecurity, and pain, God said and is saying "It is finished." The work He did at the cross does not need to be done again. Though we may be catching up to His Word, He still already did the work for us. What is left for us to do is to believe in the power of what He did. That takes us being honest with ourselves regarding where we are and allowing for our belief systems to be changed regarding what we believe about ourselves and God.

Some of us are new to this, and some of us may have been in the game a long time, but all of us must remind ourselves that it is finished. So, we may feel pain, but we have the victory over that pain through Christ. The weapons may be formed, but they will not prosper against us. Through Christ, we are victorious, and the pit cannot hold us.

This leads us to understanding our positions and posture in Christ. The first step is understanding that our salvation is necessary and needed for God to get the glory out of our lives.

Make this declaration with me: It is finished! It is finished! It is finished! The work that Jesus did on the cross is finished, and I come into agreement with every aspect of His life, death, and resurrection. Through Jesus, I have victory over every low moment or challenging season in my life. I may be going through a storm, but it does not define me because my posture of peace is found in Christ alone.

> *These things I have spoken unto you, that in me ye might have peace. In the world ye shall have tribulation: but be of*

good cheer; I have overcome the world.
~John 16:33

"The essence of our salvation is that God would be glorified in by our lives."
Victoria Orenze

Chapter 9

(The Seated Place)

Once we have revelation of God's mercy and grace towards us, the next phase is understanding our position with Him. Salvation deals with our deliverance from the consequences of sin. While we were in sin, Christ died for us so that we could have eternal life. Instead of being upset with us and not wanting to deal with us, God loved us. He took the lives that were headed towards destruction and resurrected them. Before we even entered the low places we may be experiencing, God lifted us up out of the pit and created a space for us to be seated next to Him. While we may have seasons of difficulty in life, God is with us because in the spirit, we are seated with Him in heavenly places. Check out these two passages of scripture:

So then, after the Lord had spoken to them, He was received up into heaven, and sat down at the right hand of God.

~Mark 16:19

But God, who is rich in mercy, for his great love wherewith he loved us, Even when we were dead in sins, hath quickened us together with Christ, (by grace ye are saved;) And hath raised us up together, and ***made us sit together*** *in heavenly places in Christ Jesus: That in the ages to come he might shew the exceeding riches of his grace in his kindness toward us through Christ Jesus.*

~Ephesians 2:4-7

Mark lets us know that Jesus is seated at the right hand of God. After God sent Jesus to the Earth to die for our sins, He returned to Heaven with a seat on His right-hand side prepared for His Son. That seat was a space God created for Him and only Him to occupy. There are also other seats next to Him for each of us. This is so that when we have the revelation and receive Jesus, the seat that may have been vacant can now be occupied. Make note that when I say seats here, I am more so saying this from a spiritual perspective, rather than a natural perspective, but I think picturing what it means to have a seat in the natural would be extremely helpful.

When we think of sitting down, we may overlook the details and not see the full picture. A seat has a few definitions; let's review them from the Oxford Languages Dictionary:

1. A special chair; one of recognized superiority.
2. The part of something on which one rest in sitting.
3. A seating accommodation.
4. The right to occupy such a place or a ticket indicating this right.
5. The place where something is located or based.
6. A center of authority.
7. A place of abode or residence.
8. Membership in an organization.

By defining the word seat, there were so many connections made for me that helped me to understand more about what the seated place consists of in the life of the believer. I believe that we should take a closer look at the definitions to really bring clarity to what the seated place was intended for in our lives.

1. **Special** – There is a special place for each of us to sit that only we can sit in, because that seat was created with purpose.1 Peter 2:9 reads, "But ye are a chosen generation, a royal priesthood, an holy nation, a peculiar people; that ye should shew forth the praises of him who hath called you out of darkness into his marvelous light."
2. **Rest** – Many of our spirits easily gravitate towards anxiety, but in our seated places, there is rest. We experience rest when our spirits are seated next to Jesus because there is nothing too hard for God. Matthew 11:28 reads, "Come unto me, all ye that labour and are heavy laden, and I will give you rest." Since Jesus is sitting down at the

right hand of the Father, we have the right to sit down and rest. For example, when the disciples were on the boat and the storm came, Jesus was sleeping in the bottom of the boat. The reason Jesus could sleep amid the storm was because He was already occupying His seated place.

3. **Accommodation** – An accommodation is where we live or where we reside, especially when you are on vacation. Jesus basically gave us a seat with Him and made accommodations so that we could live in this world but not be consumed by it.
4. **Right to occupy** – This place belongs to only us. Through our belief systems and relationships with God, we receive the right to occupy.
5. **Located** – The place where we are seated is next to Him. We do not have to wait until the next assignment to see that we are located in Heaven with Him. Our location is the place that we live from each day. This place should be

void of offense and unforgiveness. Where we live from each day should be a seated place of peace.

6. **Authority** – By assuming our seated places, we have positional authority based on our relationship with Jesus. Romans 8:17 reads, "Now if we are children, then we are heirs—heirs of God and co-heirs with Christ, if indeed we share in his sufferings so that we may also share in his glory." Think about a supreme court judge who has the right to a certain seat. With that seat comes a certain level of power and authority for that judge to utilize. Now, reflect on your seated place with God. There is a room with a bunch of seats, and only one for each of us. With that seat comes access and authority.
7. **Residence** – Our seated places is where we should reside every day. Our perspectives and thinking should be from our seated places. How do we live in Earth, but reside in Heaven? We maintain communion and connection

with the Father so that we can never miss a beat. By doing this, our spirits should be forever living in the seated places.

8. **Membership** – We belong to an organization; that organization is the Kingdom of God. We acknowledge our membership by having a seat in our seated places. We no longer have to search for special members-only clubs because, through Christ, we have our membership.

Picture this: A child walks into a crowded lunchroom; the child is scared and trying to find a seat. It looks like all the seats have been occupied by other children. At this point, other students may be looking at the child, wondering where the child is going to sit since every seat had already been taken up. But suddenly, a faint voice emerges from the crowd and says, "I saved a seat for you right here. Just come on over here." As the child connects with the voice, that voice becomes the most dominant voice amongst the crowd. The person then says, "I made space for you. Sit next to me." Then, the voice becomes very loud, and that's when the child traces the voice to a child a few feet away. The child pulls out a chair and waves the other child down in a crowded place.

This is us in our walks with the Lord. There is a prompting for us to follow Him, but most times, our minds and lives are crowded. As we put our attention on Him, we are fine-tuned to hear and recognize His voice. Over time, His voice becomes elevated in our spirits. The more we put attention and intention on the voice of God, the easier it is for us to rest in the finished works of Christ. We must be more intentional about finding the seats that Christ has prepared for us. We do this by studying His Word so we can better understand and recognize His voice.

Let's go back to the lunchroom. When the child sees that there is a seat being held for him or her, the child's confidence changes. Instead of feeling sad and unwanted, the child will begin to stand tall. Just think about how our spirit changes once we know that there is an accommodation already made for us in a place that is already crowded. Our whole countenance changes, and we begin to feel confident, bold, and joyful, all at the same time. This is what it's like to come into the full knowledge that God has made space for us and reserved a seat for us in His Kingdom. Not only did He reserve a seat for us, but He roped off the VIP section for each of us.

God sees us, identifies us, and says, "Son/daughter, come sit by Me." Most times, we do not realize that God has a desire for us to occupy a place with Him. A lot of times, we allow our experiences with our earthly fathers to become the lenses that we view God through, or we just allow our past hurts and traumas to get in the way of how we view the seated place.

Please know that God's desire for you to be healed, whole, financially free or to give you the desires of your heart is bigger than yours.

The Lord's heart for you is bigger than your heart for yourself, and if you will trust Him with whatever your heart is desiring, He will grant that to you if you continue to put Him first.

One important note to remember about the seated place is that there is a need for us to occupy that place with God. Our seated places are for us only. No one else can take our seats. Let's look at these scriptures to learn more about how we can occupy our seats:

> *And as they heard these things, he added and spake a parable, because he was nigh to Jerusalem, and because they thought that the kingdom of God should immediately appear. He said therefore, A certain nobleman went into a far country to receive for himself a kingdom, and to return. And he called his ten servants, and delivered them ten pounds, and said unto them,* ***Occupy till I come.*** *But his citizens hated him, and sent a message after him, saying, We will not have this man to reign over us. And it came to pass, that when he*

was returned, having received the kingdom, then he commanded these servants to be called unto him, to whom he had given the money, that he might know how much every man had gained by trading. Then came the first, saying, Lord, thy pound hath gained ten pounds. And he said unto him, Well, thou good servant: because thou hast been faithful in a very little, have thou authority over ten cities. And the second came, saying, Lord, thy pound hath gained five pounds. And he said likewise to him, Be thou also over five cities. And another came, saying, Lord, behold, here is thy pound, which I have kept laid up in a napkin: For I feared thee, because thou art an austere man: thou takest up that thou layedst not down, and reapest that thou didst not sow. And he saith unto him, Out of thine own mouth will I judge thee, thou wicked servant. Thou knewest that I was an austere man, taking up that I laid not down, and reaping that I did not sow:

Wherefore then gavest not thou my money into the bank, that at my coming I might have required mine own with usury? And he said unto them that stood by, Take from him the pound, and give it to him that hath ten pounds. (And they said unto him, Lord, he hath ten pounds.) For I say unto you, That unto every one which hath shall be given; and from him that hath not, even that he hath shall be taken away from him. But those mine enemies, which would not that I should reign over them, bring hither, and slay them before me.

~Luke 19:11-27

In this parable, Jesus talks about a ruler who comes and gives money to his servants. After giving them money, he leaves, but not before giving them one set of instructions, "Occupy until I come." When he returns, he checks with each of the servants to see what they had done with what he had given them. One servant said that he had multiplied what was given to him and now has ten pounds. The ruler then gives him authority over ten cities. The second servant says he now has five pounds above what was given. The ruler then gives him five cities. But, the last servant, when asked, said that he'd laid the pound in a napkin and saved it for the ruler. He basically buried what was given to him because of fear.

I submit to you that, upon his master's judgment, the last servant eventually found himself in the fetal position. He'd made the mistake of living his life from the fetal place. That servant allowed fear to paralyze his thinking, not being able to occupy his authority from his seated place in Christ. While it is always okay to not be okay, all of us will experience low places in our journeys, but the low place is not where we live our lives from. Even in low times, our spirits still can function in our seated places. We are still able to be connected to the Father. The beauty of our God and our Father is that He understands the process of suffering and sacrifice.

Burying what He has given to us means that we are living from the fetal position and not our God-given positions. When we bury what was given to us, we have allowed temporary emotions, experiences, or moments to attach themselves to our personalities. These moments were never meant to lead us astray and keep us out of a God-experience; they were just meant to enhance the journey. This would allow our character to be shaped, without causing us to live in a place that's less than what we are entitled to as children of God.

> *I also pray that you will understand the incredible greatness of God's power for us who believe him. This is the same mighty power that raised Christ from the dead and seated him in the place of honor at God's right hand in the heavenly realms. Now he is far above any ruler or authority or power or leader or anything else—not only in this world but also in the world to come.*
>
> *~Ephesians 1:19-21 (NLT)*

Chapter 10

(Summary)

As the song *Hold to God's Unchanging Hand* says *"Time is filled with swift transition. Naught of earth unmoved can stand. Build your hopes on things eternal. Hold to God's unchanging hand."* Life has various changes and challenges already built into our journeys. Although, we may be just coming to terms with our situations, God knew our situations before we experienced them. The important question to ask ourselves is what we are building our lives on.

My mom use to make songs out of scriptural verses. I remember the lyrics from one of the songs; she'd sang Psalms 11:3, "If the foundation be destroyed, what can the righteous do?" This verse is establishing a principle and it leads us to a pointed question—what are we building on? Are we building our lives on solid rock, or are we building on our emotions? What we build on determines what we can withstand. Let me say that differently. What we build on determines how we manage pain, transition, and grief.

There is power in taking the time to build a lasting foundation. A lasting foundation is an understanding that is built beyond what others may tell us about Jesus. It means that we seek out revelation on our own. Look at this verse discussing a parable about a man building a house.

> *He is like a man which built an house, and digged deep, and laid the foundation on a rock: and when the flood arose, the stream beat vehemently upon that house, and could not shake it: for it was founded upon a rock.*
>
> *~Luke 6:48*

This verse shares five things we must take into consideration when building:

1. **Dig deep** – When beginning to build, we first must deal with the things we have

already been taught, being ready to unlearn and relearn what we see as the truth. We must dig past traditions, prejudices, and false doctrines until we hit the solid rock that is the truth.

2. **Lay foundation** – We must lay structures that can support growth and development; this is what concretizes our faith.
3. **Build on the rock** – All structures, paths, and lanes in this building should point back to Jesus.
4. **Storm drains** – Life will bring about situations that will try to challenge our faith and our trust in Jesus. We must build filters that allow us to filter out the bad, all the while, extracting the revelation from each storm.
5. **Unshakable houses** – By being intentional about building the house, we must create homes that will not shake. We may get emotional, have our moments, or we may even visit the fetal position, but these low places will not be our homes.

By taking time to really understand the finished work of Jesus and building our faith, we can rest in the finished work of Christ Jesus. This would allow us to become steadfast and unmovable in every situation that arises. I am not saying that we will not have emotions or that we will not occasionally bend when the storms of life come our way. I am saying that we will be firmly rooted in the Word of God. In other words, we will have faith in the One who created us; this is the One who knew us before all of this began. This will make it easier to get up from the situations that we have been challenged with and enjoy the benefits found in our seated places. As the old folks would say, "This joy that I have, the world did not give it to me, and the world cannot take it away." I think what they meant by this is that what is going on around me did not give me what is inside of me, so though I may be facing some challenges, what is inside of me cannot be taken from me.

Make this final confession with me: I am what God says I am. I am not moved by what is in front of me or by what is behind me. I set my hope and expectation in the Lord. His plans for me are not meant to harm me, but to bring me to a great expected end!

> *He only is my rock and my salvation; he is my defence; I shall not be greatly moved.*
>
> *~Psalms 62:2*

Made in the USA
Middletown, DE
28 September 2022

11403945R00119